Father, Forgive

ANDREW WHITE
Father, Forgive

REFLECTIONS ON PEACEMAKING

MONARCH
BOOKS

Oxford, UK & Grand Rapids, Michigan, USA

Published by Monarch Books
an imprint of
Lion Hudson plc
Wilkinson House, Jordan Hill Road,
Oxford OX2 8DR, England
Email: monarch@lionhudson.com
www.lionhudson.com/monarch

ISBN 978 0 85721 292 4
e-ISBN 978 0 85721 466 9

First edition 2013

Acknowledgments
Scripture quotations taken from the Holy Bible,
New International Version Anglicised
Copyright © 1979, 1984, 2011 Biblica, formerly International Bible Society
Used by permission of Hodder & Stoughton Ltd, an Hachette UK company
All rights reserved
"NIV" is a registered trademark of Biblica
UK trademark number 1448790.

Scripture quotations marked "NKJV" is taken from the New King James Version.
Copyright © 1982 by Thomas Nelson, Inc. Used by permission. All right reserved.

Scripture quotation marked "NET" is from the NET Bible® copyright ©1996–2006
by Biblical Studies Press, L.L.C. http://bible.org All rights reserved. Scripture
quoted by permission.

pp. 106–109: Reproduced from the website of John Hagee Ministries. Please visit
www.jhm.org to see the full text.

Photograph 1 is used with the kind permission of Martin Williams.
Photographs 5 and 8 are used with the kind permission of Al Hassan.
All other photographs used with permission of FRRME.

A catalogue record for this book is available from the British Library

Printed and bound in the UK April 2013 (LH27).

To Justin and Caroline Welby

Contents

Acknowledgments

In giving my thanks to those who have enabled this book, I must begin by thanking those who have been part of this story of the journey of reconciliation. They have all taken great risks, endured great suffering and persevered to the end.

My warmest thanks to the Archbishop of Canterbury, the Most Revd and Rt Hon. Justin Welby. He has not only written the brilliant Foreword to this book, but he has also been my biggest partner ever in this unending journey. Together and alone we have travelled into the heart of the fire and cried, "Father, forgive."

I thank those who are part of this continuing journey with me now, both those on the ground here in the still profoundly hostile Iraq, and those who enable the work of the Foundation for Relief and Reconciliation in the Middle East in both the UK and the USA. In Baghdad I could not do my work without my immediate team, Dawood and Lina, who have been with me since they were little children. I unofficially "adopted" them over ten years ago. Now Lina is my PA and Dawood is my special assistant. They are joined by Al Hassan, my photographer and media officer, who some of the pictures for this book. Then there is Ungo, our never-failing driver, who is with us all the time. In addition to this all-Iraqi team I have our one non-local, Paul White, our Middle East Project Officer from Texas, whom I first got to know when he was a student at Wheaton College in Illinois. He travels with me wherever I am in the world.

Then there is my whole team in the UK, and especially Lesley Kent, my UK PA, Philip Rowden, Ken Phipps and all our office team. There are so many other people I need to thank who are part of this story: both political and religious leaders, as well as the various diplomats who have also supported our work.

There are two people without whom none of my books could happen: Tim Pettingale, my outstanding editor, who meticulously goes through my writing; and Tony Collins, my publisher, without whom this book simply would not have been written.

Finally, I thank the unsung heroes of my life and work – my wife Caroline and my children Josiah and Jacob – who cope without me much of the time. In essence, I can only do this work because they allow me to.

Foreword

Andrew White is one of those people that I boast of having met, and even more so boast of having worked with. He is one of the most unusual characters currently within the Church of England, defying the accusation that all ordained clergy now fit into a single mould and are without character or eccentricity.

In the eighteenth century Andrew would have been a pirate or a privateer. He has the extraordinary capacity to sail the seas of conflict, coming alongside those involved in causing and delivering violence – especially around the issues of religion – and capturing them for the cause of peace. To do this he breaks most of the rules in any book of health and safety, personal protection, and bureaucratic process.

His previous books have set out some of the stories around which he has worked. *Father, Forgive* goes back to the extraordinary events of November 1940, in which another holy pirate, the Very Revd Dick Howard, the then provost of Coventry Cathedral, went into the ruined building after the night of the first great air raid on the city of Coventry and wrote on the wall with a piece of burnt wood: "Father, forgive".

As Andrew sets out in this book that particular incident was the origin of a great movement of peace, which, under Dick Howard's successors, and those responsible for Coventry's reconciliation ministry, has led to the establishment of not far short of 200 peace centres around the world, and one of the great symbols of reconciliation. To this day, the impact of taking people to Coventry to participate in its Litany of Reconciliation, around which this book is structured, is dramatic and at times overwhelming.

Andrew is a reconciler but he never compromises with the truth of the gospel and the uniqueness of Jesus Christ. In the conclusion to this book he talks about two great commands: "Forgive, forgive, forgive", and "Love, love, love". Perhaps one of the origins of his enormous impact on those he meets is that these are genuinely the ways in which he works. He inspires forgiveness and demonstrates love, both in word and above all in action.

The Christian faith is based on the reconciliation of human beings with God through the self-giving love of Jesus. But for far too many of us that reality does not sufficiently inspire action. Andrew is one who is constantly seeking to turn reconciliation into a lived-out reality. To do that he takes huge risks, and yet the risks are taken in faith with immense determination and intelligence.

The book is controversial. There will be things in it that inspire most of us. Equally, some may disagree with something he says, but nobody can disagree with the commitment and passion with which it is written, and like all important spiritual leaders, even where there is disagreement there is also the capacity to provoke new thought, fresh imagination, and a desire to see beyond what is humanly possible to those things that are possible only with God.

The work of Coventry Cathedral continues, and Andrew is only one in a line of extraordinary individuals who have been responsible for its impact. Many have been characterized by this holy piracy, often worrying to oversee, but always deeply committed to the cause of Christ and the work of the kingdom. May the passion of this book guide our own walk with Him.

Justin Welby,
Archbishop of Canterbury

Preface

The Coventry Litany of Reconciliation

In this book I examine the wide-ranging and frequently challenging subject of reconciliation in the light of the statements set out in the Coventry Litany of Reconciliation. The Litany is loosely based on the "Seven Deadly Sins" – each of which describes an aspect of the condition of the human heart and each of which is easily identifiable as a cause of conflict in human relations. Ultimately, the Litany helps us to cut through the complex geopolitical, religious and relational quagmires that exist and get to the heart of the issue. Simply, we are all in need of reconciliation.

In *Father, Forgive* I also attempt to tackle perhaps the greatest reconciliation needed in Christianity – namely, the way in which we have dealt with the Jewish people for over 2,000 years.

But my purpose is not just to look at conflict at an international level. We must also examine our hearts as individuals. What are our own needs for personal reconciliation – not only with God but with one another?

As we come to look at reconciliation, we see that it is all to do with forgiveness. Forgiveness is the most important thing in life, since it is the only thing that can prevent the pain of the past from determining our future. So, while we look at each aspect of the Litany, remember that, in the end, forgiveness is the key to unlocking the most complex of situations.

Canon Andrew White,
Baghdad, December 2012

The Litany of Reconciliation

All have sinned and fallen short of the glory of God.

The hatred which divides nation from nation, race from race, class from class,
Father, forgive.

The covetous desires of people and nations to possess what is not their own,
Father, forgive.

The greed which exploits the work of human hands and lays waste the earth,
Father, forgive.

Our envy of the welfare and happiness of others,
Father, forgive.

Our indifference to the plight of the imprisoned, the homeless, the refugee,
Father, forgive.

The lust which dishonours the bodies of men, women and children,
Father, forgive.

The pride which leads us to trust in ourselves and not in God,
Father, forgive.

Be kind to one another, tender-hearted, forgiving one another, as God in Christ forgave you.

CHAPTER 1

From Coventry to Baghdad

At the very heart of my work is the ministry of reconciliation. Reconciliation is not an isolated event, but a continuing process; a journey. It something that cannot quickly be conjured up, but requires immense patience and nurture.

For many years now my efforts have been very much focused on and in the Middle East. This journey began for me back when I was preparing for ordination at Ridley Hall, Cambridge. I found myself being drawn into helping to restore the broken relationships between the Jews and Christians among the students at Cambridge (a story that is told in depth in *The Vicar of Baghdad*). At that time a seed was planted and from small beginnings something began to grow.

In 1998 I was appointed Director of the International Centre for Reconciliation, based at Coventry Cathedral, one of the foremost centres for reconciliation in the world. It was from here that I found myself working at an international level to help bring about reconciliation between nations and between their political leaders. The role of Coventry Cathedral in reconciliation is truly exceptional and is worth considering. It began in a remarkable way, fifty-eight years before I arrived there.

It was the night of 14 November 1940 and the Second World War was well under way. To date, no cities had been destroyed by bombing, but on this night things changed. The city of Coventry, in the heart of England, was devastated. Such was the extent of the carnage that it gave rise to the expression "coventried" – meaning to be totally destroyed.

The air raid was carried out by 515 German bombers and was codenamed Operation *Mondscheinsonate* (Moonlight Sonata). Its purpose was to destroy Coventry's factories and industrial infrastructure, but the damage to the city and its residential dwellings and monuments went far beyond this. Around 4,000 homes were destroyed and the majority of Coventry's buildings sustained some damage.

Along with this destruction came the total obliteration of its medieval Cathedral of St Michael. At around 8 p.m. it was set on fire for the first time. Volunteer firefighters managed to put out the fire, but other direct hits followed and soon new fires in the cathedral, accelerated by an internal firestorm, were out of control. A direct hit on the fire brigade headquarters disrupted the fire service's command and control, making it difficult to send fire-fighters to tackle this and the many other blazes in buildings around the city. Soon the cathedral, named after an archangel and great protector, was no more.

Standing in the midst of the still-smouldering rubble the next morning, the cathedral's leader at the time, Provost Dick Howard, took a piece of chalk and wrote on the sanctuary wall, "FATHER, FORGIVE".

People noticed that he was writing the words of our Lord from the cross. He did not write the entire phrase that Jesus spoke, however: "Father, forgive them, they know not what they do." Some wondered why the rest of the words were missing. The answer was simple: we *all* need forgiveness, not just those who had committed such an atrocity. Howard had therefore distilled the essence of Jesus' words and written the repeating heartbeat of what would become Coventry's Litany of Reconciliation. "All have sinned and fallen short of the glory of God... We also need to be forgiven," said the provost.

At the time he didn't realize how profound and prophetic his statement would prove to be. He was giving birth to an amazing ministry that would reach the ends of the earth; a pre-eminent centre for reconciliation. Howard's response, in calling for forgiveness instead of revenge, would make the ruins and the new modernist cathedral that would eventually rise up beside them, an emblem of reconciliation around the world.

A few days after the bombing, one of the cathedral staff was standing in the ruins when he noticed, lying among the rubble, the large medieval nails that had held the roof together. He took three of the nails and bound them together. This gave birth to what became known as the Coventry Cross of Nails. Today one can find hundreds of centres around the world using the cross of nails as a symbol of reconciliation. In our own church, St George's in Baghdad, a cross of nails stands on the altar, embedded in a piece of the bombed stone wall from the former cathedral. Each time I see this cross it reminds me that reconciliation is about mending that which is broken. Iraq is broken and here we are working towards its restoration. All day, every day, we are working for reconciliation.

* * *

Until I went to Coventry in 1998, much of the reconciliation work of the cathedral had focused on those who had, at one time, been in conflict with the UK. To this day, for instance, the relationship between Coventry and Dresden in Germany is outstanding. Britain led a major attack on that city in 1945, during the final few months of the Second World War. In four raids between 13 and 15 February, 722 British heavy bombers and 527 United States Army Air Force bombers dropped more than 3,900 tonnes of explosives on the city, resulting in a firestorm that destroyed fifteen square miles of the city centre and caused around 25,000 deaths. Much like Coventry, the city's cathedral, the Dresden Frauenkirche, was destroyed.

A report at the time said that the raids also destroyed 24 banks, 26 insurance buildings, 31 stores and retail houses, 640 shops, 64 warehouses, 2 market halls, 31 large hotels, 26 public houses, 63 administrative buildings, 3 theatres, 18 cinemas, 11 churches, 6 chapels, 5 other cultural buildings, 19 hospitals (including auxiliary, overflow hospitals and private clinics), 39 schools, 5 consulates, the zoo, the waterworks, the railways and 19 postal facilities.

It was often said that Dresden was destroyed in retaliation for Coventry, but the reality is that despite the severity of Coventry's destruction, it did not compare to the devastation of Dresden.

In the 1960s a group of young people went from Coventry to help rebuild the Deaconess Hospital in Dresden, which had been destroyed by British bombs. Then a group of young people from Dresden came to Coventry to help build the city's first International Centre of Reconciliation. Many years after that terrible night when the Frauenkirche was destroyed, the son of a former bomber pilot who had been a part of the raid, fashioned the cross and orb that crowned the top of this great church, restored over half a century later. Here was reconciliation in practice. The huge cross and orb stood in the nave of Coventry Cathedral before it was finally taken to Dresden.

I will never forget the great day when we handed over this incredible cross and orb. We were at the front of the church with over 100,000 people watching as the Bishop of Coventry and the cathedral canons shared in the great ceremony led by HRH the Duke of Kent. With me was my predecessor as international director at Coventry Cathedral, Canon Paul Oestreicher, who had spent a lifetime working for British–German reconciliation. Canon Paul was awarded the Order of Merit of the State of Saxony for his wonderful work of reconciliation. The links between these two cities are now so strong that whenever one is mentioned, the other comes to mind.

Although the relationship between Coventry and Dresden is unique, I have visited many places around the world that have been significantly affected by Coventry as a centre of reconciliation. The Coventry story, through the Cross of Nails ministry, has played a key role in so many other "histories", providing a beacon of hope for peace and reconciliation. For us here in Iraq, the Cross of Nails travelled to this land long before St George's was reopened in 2003. Since then, another cross has been sent here from Coventry, which was presented by Dean John Irvine to a group of our young people from Baghdad who were visiting England.

As I sit down and meet political, tribal, and religious leaders here in Baghdad, I often think to myself that it is only because of the tragedy in Coventry that I am here. All my reconciliation work in Iraq today has its foundation in the terrible night of 14 November 1940 in Coventry.

Through it I am reminded of the very foundation of our Christian faith – the miracle of resurrection; that out of death and destruction can come life, hope and a future. With Jesus we never give in, because from resurrection comes reconciliation. At the heart of Christ's resurrection was the restoration of the relationship between the Almighty and humanity – a point that St Paul makes clear in 2 Corinthians 5:16–21:

> So from now on we regard no one from a worldly point
> of view. Though we once regarded Christ in this way,
> we do so no longer. Therefore, if anyone is in Christ,
> the new creation has come: The old has gone, the
> new is here! All this is from God, who reconciled us
> to himself through Christ and gave us the ministry of
> reconciliation: that God was reconciling the world to
> himself in Christ, not counting people's sins against
> them. And he has committed to us the message of
> reconciliation. We are therefore Christ's ambassadors,
> as though God were making his appeal through us. We
> implore you on Christ's behalf: Be reconciled to God.
> God made him who had no sin to be sin for us, so that
> in him we might become the righteousness of God.

Reconciliation is central to Christian ministry. We are a new creation if we are in Christ, and through Him, God has reconciled Himself to us and, in turn, given us the ministry of reconciliation. Reconciliation is about mending that which is broken – restoring relationships to all that they were intended to be. Verse 19 makes clear that the work of reconciliation is not finished. Through His death and resurrection, Christ is still working to unite humanity with His Heavenly Father – and He accomplishes that work through us.

I don't believe that this is a ministry just for some, a special few. God has called all of us to continue the work of reconciling and restoring broken relationships at every level. It is an integral part of our remit as His ambassadors and representatives on earth. To be an ambassador is a critical and highly responsible role, since you represent your Head of State. Engaging with the British ambassador here in Iraq is part of my daily work. The speed-dial button on my telephone simply reads "HMA" (Her Majesty's Ambassador) – in other words, the person who represents the Queen. If we take seriously what St Paul says, then we are all His Majesty's Ambassadors of Reconciliation.

The phrase "Father, forgive" is such a challenging one, and yet so essential for us to both understand and practise. Jesus taught us to love our enemies and forgive those who hurt us. This is a radical, countercultural statement. Love is reconciliation in practice, because there can be no reconciliation without forgiveness. Jesus instructs us to love and forgive those who cause us pain – and healing from the pain of the past can only issue forth from forgiveness.

The biggest obstacle we have to overcome in our work of reconciliation is the people who refuse to forgive. So many wars are based simply on individuals' inability or unwillingness to forgive. If there is no forgiveness, then pain, hurt, bitterness and anger incubate in the human soul. So often, in reconciliation talks, I am presented with a long list of the hurts that the other party has caused to that person, people-group or nation. Stored-up pain causes immense conflict and division.

Yet, the principle of "Father, forgive" provides a way out of this trap. As Jesus taught us, forgiveness is the key that unlocks so much potential in the Christian life. Forgiveness releases people who are trapped in the past to become all they were intended to be, now in the present and in the future. If hope can arise from situations as terrible as Coventry and Dresden, then it can arise for each of us. Out of pain and even death can come healing and reconciliation. Three nails wrought into a cross – forgiveness, reconciliation and hope. We are indeed privileged to serve Christ in the ministry of resurrection.

CHAPTER 2

We All Need Restoration

All have sinned and fallen short of the glory of God.

As we begin to think about the need for and practice of reconciliation, we do so by recognizing that, ultimately, we all need to be reconciled to God. We all begin our life journeys from the same position – one of being inadequate in our relationship with the Almighty. Fundamental reconciliation happens when our relationship with God is restored and we become followers and lovers of Jesus. We all need to know God and love Him.

Central to our faith is John 3:3: "no one can see the kingdom of God unless they are born again." This passage is all about reconciliation. The deepest need of every human is to be brought into a right relationship with their Creator. In Christian circles we talk about the need to be "saved" and what it means to be "born again" – to be renewed and have our broken relationship with God restored.

In the Western Church most people remember very clearly the day when they gave their heart to Jesus and were reconciled to God. Here in Iraq, it is not always so clear. I remember one of our Iraqi young people telling me that while he was visiting England, "All these people told us about when they *became* Christians. Were they not born Christian?" This is a fundamental difference between Iraq and the West. Most Christians in Iraq are born into Christian families. From the time of their birth they are taken to church and are taught to love Jesus. They know He is real and never doubt Him. They are often a persecuted minority, but they know that in all they experience, their Lord is with them.

This is a very different approach to the Western Church's view of faith and salvation, yet it is totally in line with my own personal experience. One of the earliest childhood memories I have is of being taught that Jesus loves me. With childlike simplicity, because Jesus loved me, I loved Him back, and the experience of His love was very real. Why complicate matters further than this? It did not matter to me as a young child that I could not see Jesus; I knew that He was real. I loved Him like I loved my own mother and father, and I knew that He never left me. I would talk to Him throughout my day and He was my closest and best friend.

As a child I recall being told in Sunday school that I had to "give my heart" to Jesus. Since my relationship with Him was so real already, I had no idea what this meant. I tried (in vain, because I could never quite get it right) to cut out a literal heart shape from paper, so that I could somehow "give" this to Him. It wasn't until I was much older that I understood that what the phrase was referring to was the relationship that I already had with my God. I had always loved Him and always would.

While it is always wonderful to hear the many incredible stories of people's conversions, I do not have one. But although I never had a "conversion experience", I do have the experience of the Jesus who has never left me. My experience is the same as that of so many people in St George's, Baghdad. They have known the immense love of Jesus from birth and love Him dearly.

The love of Christ must be the starting point for reconciliation. It is His love alone which has the power to bring healing to a broken world. Only love can form the foundation of real, lasting reconciliation. Jesus' message to the world was *love, love, love.* He taught us to "Love the Lord your God with all your heart and with all your soul and with all your strength and with all your mind" and to "Love your neighbour as yourself" (Luke 10:27). Then He called us to radical love: "Love your enemies and pray for those who persecute you" (Matthew 5:44). This is so contrary to the way in which most people think and behave. How can you love those who have stolen from you, assaulted or abused you, or tried to blow you up and completely destroy you? How can you forgive those who have kidnapped, tortured and killed someone you love? Yet, this is where reconciliation has to begin. Since I have lived in Iraq, I have come to understand, on a completely new level, that the Coventry Litany of Reconciliation is not just a good idea, not just sound theological theory, but that it encompasses a potent, life-changing truth which, if lived out, has the power to transform both the person who acts upon it and the lives of countless others around them.

The Litany begins with the words, "All have sinned and fallen short of the glory of God." Provost Howard's words were profound when he inscribed "Father, forgive" on the sanctuary wall, rather than "Father, forgive them..." It is not just *them* who are in need of forgiveness. We all need it!

In Iraq, Jesus' radical challenge to forgive those who mean us harm is not an occasional challenge, but a daily one. Forgiveness is a constant, continuous act of the will – something we walk out and practise regularly. In early November 2012 a terrible bomb explosion in Baghdad killed more than sixty, including several people who were very close to me. I recorded the following in my diary a week or so later:

The Middle East continues to be in turmoil. As I watch television I see stories of killings in Gaza, Israel and Syria. Such terrible news. 40 people killed in Gaza, 3 in Israel and 9 in Syria... By 12.00pm today there had been serious bombings and 119 people had been killed. Just as we were about to go to our service I wrote the following on my Facebook page:

"We are about to go and worship now. God has not left us, though everybody else has. We have just had 119 people killed in two terrible car bombs and you do not see even one line about it in any of the international media.

"Our people are really frightened and feel forgotten. People have started fleeing again in their masses, things are just so bad. People have nothing. One of our staff saw one of our congregation begging on the street yesterday. He asked her why she was doing this. She said all the food she had from the church had run out and she has no money to pay her rent. We will give her everything she needs today, but it is another example of the terrible need here. All may have left us but our Lord is still here.

"None of our people were caught in the bombings, but things have really deteriorated in Baghdad. The violence is so terrible that, once again, we are seeing many of our own people fleeing to Turkey and Lebanon. We have not seen people fleeing the country like this for several years. The fact is, we were warned by one of the most senior religious leaders that this was being planned. Iraq is no longer a news issue. We cannot blame the media for this. So many of the journalists have been targeted here and many killed, especially locals. The media have moved on to the traumas elsewhere in the region.

"Our gospel reading today was from Mark 13. In it Jesus tells His disciples that before the Second Coming there will be wars and rumours of wars. Well, we have sure got them. But our congregation took hope in this, because soon and very soon we are going to see the KING."

It is so difficult, when you have been hurt, to meet with those who know the people who have hurt you. The people who *know* those who have committed the violence will often visit me at St George's to plan how we can work together for reconciliation. When a terrible massacre of Christians happened at the end of 2010, one of the top Sunni sheikhs came and spoke at our church. In the service he condemned what had happened and assured everyone that he was their brother. As people stood and clapped the sheikh it was clear that they too were one with him.

He returned for our curate's ordination as a priest. This time he said nothing but just sat quietly in the service. At times there is no need for words when one is working for reconciliation: your presence says enough.

If we pause to look at ourselves, we realize how ill equipped and inadequate we are without the Lord's help. It is so easy to look at others and focus on their inadequacies, rather than beginning with ourselves. At the heart of conflict is the mis-truth that it is always someone else who is the problem. It always grieves me when I see how much time people in church spend arguing with one another, or worse, telling other church members that all their problems are being caused by a particular person. We cannot even think about being ambassadors of reconciliation if we have not realized that often we are the ones who are sinning and causing division, especially among the people of God, His Church. I have to be honest; I have so often found it easier to work through reconciliation issues with non-Christians.

At the same time, I have to confess that my trust in the Church has been so greatly enhanced by living with my people here at St George's in Baghdad. Here our people have nothing, most have lost everything, yet the presence of Jesus is so real. We talk about love all the time, and in love we see the beginning of reconciliation. The glory or miraculous presence of God is a constant topic of conversation. God is ever present in His power and majesty, and in times of distress the Holy Spirit provides comfort and, truly, a peace that transcends the rational.

To be constantly immersed in God's glory is something we strive for, given the words of the Litany which echo Romans 3:23. We have "fallen short of the glory of God". These words form the bedrock of both my calling and my work in reconciliation. Recognizing that I myself have sinned and fallen short of God's glorious standards means that when I approach situations in which reconciliation is needed, I am acutely aware that progress can only be made through and because of the glory of God and His mercy and grace.

I recall once being asked why it is that I speak so much about the glory of God and not His Kingdom. It is simply because I am totally reliant on the glory – the presence of God. My own resources are woefully inadequate to attempt many of the things I'm called upon to do. As I sit down opposite individuals, some of whom may be involved in extreme violence, I am keenly aware that what I am trying to accomplish in terms of working towards a place of peace and reconciliation is only possible through the power and glory of God. Holiness and the power of the Holy Spirit are my only tools for this work. The power of our Lord is supernatural and really works in reconciliation. I cannot stand up in our gatherings and say these words, but I can pray them. In very political and diplomatic contexts, I know where my power and direction come from. It is not from me.

So in the midst of the highly complex work of reconciling enemies who are motivated to kill one another, I realize that, of myself, I can do nothing. But through the power and the glory of Jesus I can do everything. Jesus can bring hope into situations where none exists. Jesus can sow the seeds of His love into situations where there is only fear, mistrust and hatred. We have all fallen short of the glory of God, but it is His glory that brings about the change. When the need for reconciliation is so apparent, and many before have tried and failed to bring about peace, I simply pray, "Lord, come in your glory."

CHAPTER 3

A Divided World

The hatred which divides nation from nation, race from race, class from class,

Father, forgive.

Reconciliation is needed wherever division exists. The reasons for division are usually complex and difficult to untangle, but the task of reconciliation is always to heal the rift caused by conflict; to help people to understand one another's different perspectives and work to restore peace.

Simply put, reconciliation is healing something that has been torn apart.

Almost every problem, regardless of its scale or complexity, can be distilled down to division – whether the root cause is a divergence of political policy, a strong religious, ideological or philosophical disagreement or, as we shall see later, a number of other factors rooted in the selfishness of the human heart.

At a global level, we have seen the traditional hatred towards the Jewish people revealed through anti-Semitism, division between Eastern and Western nations, division between Arabs and Jews or, here in Iraq, division between Shia and Sunni. This is not to mention the dividing issues around the world that surround class, educational and political systems. Such divisions do not always result in violent behaviour, but often they do, as one party struggles to enforce their view over their opponent's view.

Apart from my involvement in St George's, Baghdad, much of my work is related to religious sectarianism, bringing together those who have traditionally been enemies. In this capacity I chair the High Council of Religious Leaders in Iraq. The sad fact is, religion is very much tied up with violence. As Archbishop William Temple said during the Second World War, "When religion goes wrong, it goes very wrong." The apostle John, recording the words of Jesus in his Gospel, wrote, "the time is coming when anyone who kills you will think they are offering a service to God. They will do such things because they have not known the Father or me" (John 16:2–3). This is what we have witnessed in our time.

In this chapter I want to look at some of the multitude of divisions between people groups that have arisen around the world – first, those that are found in Iraq, my adopted home, and then others in various places in the world. I want to examine some of the issues involved and the problems they create.

One of the greatest divisions has been between Jews and Christians. Partly because this is a large, complex issue and partly because it was instrumental in first drawing me into the work of reconciliation, I have dedicated several chapters to examining it. Other situations are not dealt with in the same depth.

Christian and Muslim

The division between Christians and Muslims has become one of the biggest sources of tension in the world today and is, perhaps, the division which receives the most media attention. In some places the tension has spilled over into violence. We also know only too well about the acts of terrorism committed by Muslim extremists, resulting in the deaths of many. At the outset, two things must be recognized here:

1. This violence is committed by just a tiny minority of Muslims. Most Muslims are our friends. The only way to stop violence being committed against Christians is to engage with those committing the violence. Much of the work of reconciliation has to be conducted face to face with those who are, themselves, committing violent acts.

2. We have to recognize that, historically, a greater number of Muslims have been killed in the name of Christianity by those who called themselves

Christians, than the number of Christians who have been killed by Muslims. This is a sad fact of history.

Showing love to Muslims does not mean having to compromise our faith and love for Jesus – something that seems to puzzle or confuse many Christians. He is our Lord, our Master and the one we love. Perhaps the most important aspect of reconciliation is simply showing love to another. This initially sounds easy, but can be incredibly difficult when it means being Christlike towards someone who is full of evil and violence – those who have fought our people, sometimes killed our people and often massacred huge numbers of innocents. But reconciliation must have a starting point. It may be a long, uphill struggle to close a historic rift, but the process of reconciliation must begin somewhere. Usually that means establishing some common ground. Before you can do anything, you must become "friends" with your enemy. You do this by showing them unconditional love.

The American poet Longfellow said, "Who is my enemy? It is the person whose story I have not heard." This statement is profoundly true. Hearing people's stories is one of the things that I so often try to do.

In my efforts to bring about religious reconciliation in the Middle East, I have often begun the work by getting various sides to simply listen to one another's stories. One reconciliation conference I hosted involved bringing together twelve different people in a hotel for three days. I had set aside one whole day for us just to listen to one another's stories. I felt quietly impressed with myself for allocating such a generous amount of time for simply listening.

We listened, listened and listened, but it soon became clear that we had hardly begun. The entire three days passed by, and we were still listening. We hadn't come anywhere close to being ready to move on. Two months later we met again and the same thing happened. We met again and again.

In the end, it took almost two years of spread-out meetings before every person had had the opportunity to express all they needed to say. And I thought we could accomplish this in one day! I learnt so much from this mistake. To *really* listen to another person's story, so that they are no longer our enemy and therefore distant from us, takes time; a *lot* of time. But with commitment and persistence, over time and with mutual understanding, enemies can become friends.

In order to be able to work towards reconciliation between Muslims and Christians, two basic elements must be in place.

First, as above, there must be the willingness to truly listen to the other party and hear what they are saying – even if we do not like what they are saying.

Second, we have to be willing to make compromises. There must be a sense that both sides are willing to give some ground in order to move forward and "meet" the other person. It is essential, though, that our motives for reconciliation are pure and that our expression of love is sincere, accompanied by practical demonstrations. Otherwise, we can say what we like, but we will not be taken seriously.

When we first formed our foundation, it was called simply The Foundation for Reconciliation in the Middle East. We soon changed the name by adding to "Reconciliation" the word "Relief". It was important that the people we were reaching out to knew that we wanted to do something practical to help their situation – not just persuade them to see things differently.

If you are going to provide relief for someone, you first need to know what kind of needs they have. The needs in Iraq are clear. People need healthcare, food, education and housing. Through our church in Baghdad we have sought to provide for all of these needs, and we have made clear that this provision is not just for our own people, but also for people of any faith. We have a large clinic seeing over 150 patients a day with a dentist, doctors, a pharmacy, a laboratory, an X-ray unit and a haematology unit. All treatments are provided totally free of charge and 95 per cent of our patients are not Christians. Occasionally I am called into the clinic to help insert intravenous lines when the staff have failed to cannulate their patients. This takes me back to my pre-ordained life when I worked in the field of anaesthesia. For me, putting in intravenous lines is like riding a bike – you never forget how to do it!

In addition to our clinic, we also have a very modern infant school and a major food relief programme to help the many poor of our community. The Islamic community can therefore see that we provide real help and honestly care for everyone. The result has been that Islamic community leaders see us as friends and not foes. Here is reconciliation in process. By acts of practical love and real listening we have made a difference to how we are seen, and now we are listened to. This approach has laid a real foundation for our work in reconciliation.

Sunni and Shia Islam

A large part of my work nowadays is concerned with reconciliation between Shia and Sunni. The conflict between the two has been widely publicized, yet the vast majority of people in the West are not aware of the differences between these two groups. I therefore want to go into some detail about these two major strands of Islam, so that people understand the fundamentals of the issue.

In Christian terms, the difference can be seen as similar to the difference between Catholic and Protestant: two strands with similar creeds. Catholic and Protestant used to kill each other regularly not so long ago, and sadly, we have seen similar violence and murder between Sunni and Shia.

Both groups are Muslims, so fundamentally they share the same Islamic beliefs. Over the years, the two traditions have developed different practices in several respects, and these in turn are seen as carrying certain spiritual implications. The two traditions' differences are not primarily theological, however, but concern their origins. These date back to the very beginning of Islam and are to do with who was identified as the true successor of Mohammed.

There were those who thought that the leadership of Islam should be placed under the control of the companions of Mohammed, who were proven, capable leaders. There were twelve people who were seen as the right leadership team, and these became known as the Caliphs. Those who held to this position gave birth to the group that became known as the Sunnis.

They were originally led by Abu Bakr. The Sunni see themselves as orthodox, traditional Muslims. Their practices regarding prayer, pilgrimage and fasting differ significantly from those of Shia Islam. The word "Sunni" comes from *Ahl al-Sunna*, which literally means "the people of the tradition".

In Shia Islam, they believe that the role of leadership passed down the hereditary line from Mohammed through his son-in-law, Imam Ali. For the Sunni, however, the successor of Mohammed was not Imam Ali but clearly the twelve caliphs.

The Sunni consider that their tradition is closer to that

of Mohammed and the prophets mentioned in the Quran. Though Mohammed is seen as the final prophet, there are other people who are very important to the Shia, such as Imams Ali and Husain (though they are not considered to be as central as Mohammed).

There is another practical distinction: the Sunni have traditionally come under state control while in reality, in countries such as Iraq and Iran, the Shia clerics are the real, ultimate authority.

The vast majority of Muslims are Sunni (about 85 per cent in global terms), so overall Shia Muslims are a minority, but Shia form the majority in Iran, Iraq, Bahrain and Yemen.

Central to Shia beliefs are the historic Imams. They are seen as being sinless in their very essence because of their holy lineage, with total authority coming from Allah. The historic Imams are venerated like saints and their tombs are venerated as shrines. Pilgrimage to these shrines is a very regular occurrence.

As I have explained, Shias trace their line back to Imam Ali. He was both the cousin and son-in-law of Mohammed. He was seen as the rightful heir of Mohammed. Great significance is attached to the lineage of Imam Ali. Anybody in his line is called a Sayed (Sir), and to this day all the Imams of this lineage wear a black rather than a white turban. The colour black is of great importance to the Shia: it is the colour of mourning for those in one's own family, and since they are still mourning the death of Ali and his grandson Husain – considered to be the two greatest leaders of their own family – it is highly appropriate that the turban should be coloured black. The West is not very aware of Shia Islam. Shias are often referred to as "Shia militia". They are known as the militants who control Iran and have carried out negative activity in Lebanon. But the fact is, the majority of the Shia are a peaceful and wonderful people. As a church, our relationship to them is particularly close.

Shia Islam operates within a highly hierarchical structure, where orders are passed down from the grand ayatollah Ali Al Sistani, based in Najaf – a very holy Shia town in Iraq where Imam Ali is buried and has his shrine. The Majoria, the other four grand ayatollahs, who are next in line to Ali Al Sistani, surround the grand ayatollah.

During one particular onslaught against the Christians in Iraq, the Shia offered the Christians sanctuary and protection. The general feeling among the Christians is that the Shia will protect them. Most of the recent attacks on Christians have come from a very small section of the Sunni.

Reconciliation between Shia and Sunni is key to the future of Iraq. There are extremists in both groups. Their divide dates back over 1,000 years, but today it is deeper than ever.

Much of our work has been in bringing these two strands of Islam together, despite their centuries of strife. The leaders of these groups are the people I mentioned earlier, who have listened to one another for more than two years and have gradually learnt to trust one another enough to become friends. They trust us, and we continue to demonstrate practical love to them. At one level, the reconciliation process is working.

The vast majority of violence in Iraq is perpetrated by people who carry out their terrorism to justify their religious stance. If you examine the position of each group, it is clear that they commit the violence because they have a profound sense of loss. The major leader of the Sunnis in Iraq, a great man of peace who I work with continually, is Sheikh Khalid. He has often said to me that 80 per cent of the violence is carried out by people from his own tradition. It cannot be denied that the Sunni community has lost the most since the war in 2003. Saddam was a Sunni, and since the war this group of people has lost a great deal through the process of "deBa'athification": money, property, industry, employment, but ultimately power. They are therefore opposed to the Shia majority and against any who are seen as being part of the group who led the war in 2003 – the Americans, the British and the other countries of the original coalition.

The leaders of this terrorist movement are not even from Iraq; they are mainly from the surrounding Arab nations. Here in Iraq they are simply known as AQI (Al Qaeda Iraq). They have sought to get Sunni Iraqis to support them and to carry out much of the work on the ground. AQI got the support of many of the Sunnis living in the predominantly Sunni district of Al Anbar. The Sunnis were paid by AQI, who gave them the support to carry out the worst of the suicide bombings. Then another group came along who needed the Sunnis of Al Anbar. This group was none other than the US Army, which was offering more payment to join a group called the Sons of Iraq, and their job was to work for peace. It was while this group was functioning after 2007 that we saw a major fall in violence. Since the 'S withdrawal in 2011 we have once again seen a steady increase in violence.

As mentioned, it has been suggested that 80 per cent of all suicides are the work of the Sunnis. This shows two major issues are at play here: first, that the Sunnis are responsible for much of the violence; second, that you cannot buy those involved in this violence – you can only hire them.

A particularly sad development was the formation of groups such as "the Birds of Paradise" around the northern town of Kirkuk. This was a group of children aged between nine and thirteen. They were trained to be suicide bombers because, as children, they were less likely to have to undergo intense security checks that would expose their evil intent. More recently a new group has been established, based in Hilla, the modern town of Babylon. The group, called "the Fourth Brigade", is also made up of children, but this time they are even younger, aged from seven to thirteen. Once again, this group appears to be the work of AQI.

The main work of the Fourth Brigade has not even begun yet, but of particular concern this time is that those involved are supposedly targeting Christians.

Iraqi Christians are seen as being linked to the West. The fact is that there have been Christians in Iraq for more years than most other places in the world. It is an acknowledged fact that monotheistic religion in Iraq began with the arrival of Jonah in Nineveh, followed by the work of the prophet Nahum. The people of this city were the Assyrians, and they started to believe in the God of Abraham, Isaac and Jacob. Seven hundred years later somebody else turned up on his way to India – here he is much revered and is simply known as Mar Thoma. He asked the people of Nineveh if they knew that the Messiah had come. They said that they did not, so he told them, and they believed. To us in the West, this man is known as Doubting Thomas. To this very day, 2,700 years after Jonah, most of the Christians in Iraq (and my entire congregation) are originally from the city of Nineveh. They are still known simply as the Assyrians, the bad people who became good.

I get very frustrated when I hear that what is needed is simply advocacy with governments, diplomats and foreign ministries. These people, in a direct sense, can do nothing about such crises, but what they can do is put pressure on governments to support organizations like ours and fund our engagement in such work. We were very fortunate to win the support of the Danish Government, who have funded our efforts. What made the difference was that the people we were dealing with knew the people committing the violence and could exert pressure on them to observe the fatwa and curtail the aggression of those causing violence. (A fatwa is a major religious injunction and it cannot be ignored when put together by the senior Islamic leaders – both Sunni and Shia. The nearest thing to a fatwa in Christian terms would be a papal injunction being given by the Catholic pope.) What came out of the meeting in Copenhagen was complex intelligence that I cannot share here, but we managed to have a very productive meeting between all the relevant coalition ambassadors and our delegates.

Muslims and Yazidi

Of all the minorities in Iraq, the Yazidi have suffered the most. The reason for this is their complex belief system, which is viewed by others as being non-monotheistic. The nearest religious group to them is probably the Zoroastrians. Many view them as devil worshippers. In the Yazidi belief system, God created the world and it is now in the care of a group of seven holy beings, often known as Angels or *heft sirr* (the Seven Mysteries). Pre-eminent among these is Tawûsê Melek (Melek Taus in English), the Peacock Angel. You will see this "angel" appearing regularly in the architecture of their main place of worship in Kurdistan. The reason for the Yazidi's reputation as devil worshippers is that Melek Taus is also referred to as Shaytan – the Quran's name for Satan. The Yazidi community is now very small. Their main base is Iraq but they are also found in Syria, Iran, Turkey and Armenia, and they quote the size of their worldwide community as being between 50,000 and 500,000. The true number is probably on the lower end of that range.

They have many strange practices. For example, they avoid the colour blue and never eat lettuce. They are a very closed community. People are not allowed to leave the community or marry out of it. The community killed one of its young women recently when she got engaged to a Muslim.

In recent years the Yazidi community has suffered a great deal. On 14 August 2007 over 500 of them were killed in the largest single suicide bombing against any community, with two coordinated truck bombs. Attacks on this community continue to take place.

It is difficult to understand much about their practice of faith. When I asked their top Sheikh how they worship, all he could tell me was that on Tuesdays they stand outside and look up at the sun. Here in Iraq they come from the same place as many of the Christians, the Nineveh Plains. Their relationship with the Christians is stable. They are such a closed community that I have never met anyone who knows very much about them. In terms of our reconciliation work, our efforts have simply been to make friends with them and to begin to broker relationships between their leaders and the Muslims on the High Council. Despite the aggressive attitudes of many Muslims towards the Yazidi, the High Council leaders are befriending them and recognize the need to protect all Iraqi minority groups.

Mandaeans

The Mandaeans are one of the smallest minority groups in Iraq. Followers of Mandaeanism revere Adam, Abel, Seth, Enosh, Noah, Shem, Aram and especially John the Baptist, but reject Jesus and Christianity. They are sometimes identified in connection with the Sabian religion mentioned in the Quran. Most scholars say that the Mandaeans migrated to Mesopotamia from the Southern Levant and are of pre-Arab and pre-Islamic origin. In modern-day Iraq they are simply known as the followers of John the Baptist and are recognized for their practices. The Mandaeans take baptism beyond its original intention to another degree of ritual. They not only marry in water, but have their weekly act of worship in water as well. I always say they are far more Baptist than the Baptists! When I first met with their spiritual leader a few years ago, he assured me that their community was thousands of years old and had existed long before John the Baptist, but every community here claims to be ancient.

Tribes

In Iraq tribal divisions are taken very seriously and disputes can arise between one tribe and another. Tribes are larger than family groupings and are usually linked to a particular area or location: for example, the Najafi tribe from Najaf, and the Falluji tribe from Fallujah in the Iraqi province of Al Anbar. Tribal divisions are an issue here, but not on the same scale as in parts of Africa, where there is often major conflict between tribes.

Westerners should not look down on tribal divisions. Those who believe that there are no such things as tribes in the West are mistaken. Our varied backgrounds mark us out as belonging to one tribe or another, just as much as anywhere else in the world. Many of our Western societal divisions would be viewed as tribal divisions by those in other parts of the world. There are major divisions surrounding the issues of race and class. In Britain the class divides are bigger than in many other countries. People want to know: Are we from the right kind of family background? What school and university did we go to? This even spills over into faith: What denomination do we come from, or what church do we belong to within our denomination?

Arabs and Israel/Jews

In the context of this book I won't attempt to address this highly contentious and sensitive issue. Hostilities have broken out once again, even as I write. An entire book would not do the topic justice, let alone a few paragraphs. I lived and worked in Israel and the Palestinian Authority areas for many years. I will touch on the issue again later in the chapters regarding Jewish/Christian relations. The central point that must be grasped by all who want to understand this complex issue is that Israel is a land that is called "holy", and yet all of its peoples are suffering minorities.

The Jews may be a majority population in Israel, but they are only a minute community of no more than 13 million in the whole world. Despite being a highly successful, academic, and influential people, they remain a tiny minority. They have also suffered more than any other people group, with 6 million being killed in the last world war alone, and hundreds of thousands killed around the world in the last 2,000 years.

Equally, the Muslim Arabs in Israel have suffered like no other Arabs in the Middle East. They have not only been caught up in countless conflicts, but have also lost property, territory, at times influence and ultimately power.

The Christian Arabs in Israel have become the minority of minorities. They too have lost all of the above. Many of them have left the country, and in the Palestinian areas many have suffered persecution.

Theological differences within religions

As well as the divisions that exist between diverse groups with clear ideological or theological differences, divisions can also exist within the same group. Christians speak frequently about the need for unity but, sadly, they can be as divided as any other religion regarding differences in theology and practice. Many Western Christians seem to find it hard to cope with the fact that unity does not mean uniformity and that diversity can exist within unity. They tend to want to persuade other Christians to see things exactly as they do when it comes to their interpretation of the Scriptures. Some are so dogmatic that if people don't agree with them, they are viewed as misguided or even far from God. Trying to bring about reconciliation between such parties is difficult – perhaps more difficult than reconciling enemies who have been at war with one another. But it will always be difficult to help people to consider the viewpoints of others when they believe they have a direct mandate from God.

Orthodox and Catholic

This is not to mention the major divide within Christianity between Catholics and Protestants. Historically, the results of this have been as traumatic as the results of the divide between Shia and Sunni. People often ask, "Why are the Muslims killing each other?" But the fact is, ever since the division of the Church into its Eastern and Western branches in 1054, there has been serious conflict. This is referred to as the East–West Schism or the Great Schism.

A delegation was sent from Rome insisting that the pope should be recognized as the head of all the churches. Cardinal Humbert, leading the delegation, excommunicated the Patriarch of Constantinople when he refused to submit to the pope. The patriarch in turn excommunicated Cardinal Humbert. This was just the beginning of a 100-year conflict, which eventually led to a total schism.

In the last few years major reconciliation has taken place, but only after a thousand years of division. The first significant act of reconciliation came in 1991 when the Ecumenical Patriarch of Constantinople visited the Vatican for the first time. Pope John Paul II and the patriarch both said they wished to dismiss the past edicts of excommunication and to re-establish full communion with each other. On 29 June 2004, at the great feast of St Peter and St Paul, the Ecumenical Patriarch Bartholomew went to the Vatican and shared in the great liturgy with Pope John Paul II. Here was a genuine re-enactment of our Lord's words: "Father, forgive..."

The hatred which divides nation from nation, race from race, class from class,

Father, forgive.

I could have catalogued so many more divisions that exist around the world, but I have limited my comments to the areas I know best. In so many places animosity continues between neighbouring people groups. We remind ourselves that reconciliation is needed wherever division exists.

CHAPTER 4

The Rift Begins: Jews and Christians

If one were to ask, "Where is the greatest division today?", there are many things that could be said: "Jew and Arab" or "Muslim and Jew" would be high on the list. Others may say, "Christians and Muslims". The reality of these divisions cannot be denied. The fact is, though, that one of the biggest divisions in history has existed between two people groups who come from the same roots: Jews and Christians.

More Jews have been killed at the hands of Christians than any other religious group by another. Jews and Christians have so much in common and yet, historically, there has been so much hatred between the two. Christianity grew out of the same roots as Judaism:

both faiths see Abraham as their father. The founder and leader of Christianity was a Jew, Jesus of Nazareth. Christianity began as a sect of Judaism. Yet over time, anti-Semitic attitudes have arisen among Christians and an anti-Judaic polemic was formed that persists today. It is a polemic that not only affected Christianity, but also grew in the lands that called themselves Christian.

I grew up in an environment that was philo-Semitic. As a young child I remember being taught many positive things about the Jews. I was taught that our faith came out of Judaism and was warned about the dangers of anti-Semitism. I grew up close to a Jewish cemetery and was aware that, from time to time, people would attack the cemetery and even destroy the graves. One of my earliest childhood memories of dressing up and play-acting was pretending to be a policeman who was guarding the Jewish cemetery. No doubt many would view my childhood as a bit strange, but as a young boy my reading matter was predominantly medical textbooks and books on Judaism.

As an adult, when I finally left the medical world to train for ordination at Cambridge, I thought this would be a great opportunity to learn more about Judaism, and indeed it was. Apart from the study of Christian theology, Judaism was the subject I adored, and I attended numerous lectures on the subject by my favourite scholar, Nicholas de Lange, who was both a rabbi and a professor. It was he who suggested that a good way for us, as theological students, to really understand Judaism was to go and visit the student synagogue in Thompson's Lane, Cambridge.

I went along and soon became a regular Friday night attendee. I loved the worship, and after the service we would eat a wonderful kosher meal together. It was not long before I realized that most of my friends were Jewish.

I also, of course, attended the Christian Union. Every three years the CU held a major mission to try to convert as many students as possible. One year, the mission committee was chaired by my good friend Richard Coombes. Richard lived in the room next door to me at Ridley Hall, Cambridge, and would eventually be the best man at my wedding.

One year the CU agreed that the missionary organization Jews for Jesus would be invited, so that Jewish students specifically could be targeted. The Jewish students were naturally in uproar about this. As the only Christian who was a regular attendee of the synagogue and a member of the Jewish Society, it was presumed that I was the person to do something about this.

The headline of the *Jewish Chronicle* one week simply read: "Holy War in Cambridge". I spent many hours bringing together the Jewish and Christian student communities. They listened intently to each other. Eventually, it was decided that we needed to form an actual society to bring Jews and Christians together. It was called CUJAC: Cambridge University Jews and Christians.

Eventually the CU mission meeting with Richard Harvey, the representative of Jews for Jesus, did go ahead. The room was filled to overflowing with members of our newly formed CUJAC and of the Jewish Society. The speaker stated that no meeting he had ever conducted had received so much publicity! The meeting was polite, though the Jewish students made clear their anger and opposition to it.

The opposition to the meeting by Jewish students was based on a fear that was not just contemporary, but rooted in 2,000 years of mistrust and misunderstanding. Personally, I was doing more than just gaining a new understanding of Judaism – the foundation was being laid for the rest of my life.

It was not long before I took some time away from my Cambridge-based studies to study in Jerusalem. First I studied at the Hebrew University in Jerusalem and then at an ultra-Orthodox Yeshiva (seminary) in the extremely Orthodox area of Jerusalem called Mea Shearim.

To this day I see this experience as one of the most important of my life. Here I did not just begin to understand Judaism, I began to live it. Here, I also began to gain my love for the Middle East and my hatred of all anti-Judaic polemic. It does not take long in one's study of Judaism to realize that it cannot be understood purely from books. To be truly understood, it has to be lived. This was what I was beginning to do. The fact that our faith came from Judaism meant that there was no contradiction between my beliefs and the Torah. Now, so much of what I had learnt and studied came to life. What I had learnt from the Hebrew Scriptures no longer seemed distant. Rather, it became both clear and relevant. My love was clearly for Judaism and Israel, but this was also my introduction to the Middle East which was to shape me and eventually become the reason why I am now based in Baghdad, though still working in Israel most months.

The division begins

When Judaism actually began is a debatable issue. Some Jews will argue that it has existed from creation, but many more will point to Abraham, the father of the faith and the one who is viewed as the father of all three monotheistic faiths. It was he who travelled from Ur (in modern-day Iraq) to Canaan (modern-day Israel), where Judaism was established as a faith and a people.

There are those who say that Judaism was not established until Moses, when the Law was given. This argument does not easily hold up, as the Hebrew people were already a clearly identifiable ethnic group, and thus were experiencing their first exile at the hand of the Pharaoh in Egypt.

Throughout the history of the Jewish people, from the very beginning, they have endured endless suffering. Sadly, it is after the division between Judaism and early Christianity that we begin to see a theological justification for anti-Judaic polemic, which eventually became violent.

In its very beginnings, Christianity saw itself as intrinsically linked to Judaism. Most of its members were Jews. Christians followed a Jew whom they saw as the Messiah, the anointed one of God, who always made clear that His message was first for the Jew, as Paul points out: "For I am not ashamed of the gospel of Christ, for it is the power of God to salvation for everyone who believes, for the Jew first and also for the Greek" (Romans 1:16 NKJV).

Early Christianity saw itself as a sect within Judaism and never as a "new religion". At no time did Jesus ever imply that He was not a Jew or that He had started a new religion. Jesus was soon seen as a divine figure as well as the one who had fulfilled the messianic expectations of those who followed Him. It was after the departure of Jesus that the tension really began.

As more Gentiles became followers of Jesus, there was increasing tension regarding which *halachich* (Jewish legal traditions) had to be followed. The big question was, to what extent did one need to follow Judaism in order to follow Jesus? This included major issues such as circumcision – something that Paul dealt with in depth.

The issue of the role of Paul with regard to Judaism is still very much debated. On one hand, he is seen as being one of the main proponents of developing a non-legalistic Christianity. At the same time, he made clear his own Jewish tradition and emphasized the close relationship between Judaism and Christianity. He made clear in Romans 9–11 that the Church could not boast or claim any superiority over Israel, because Israel was its root.

Very early on, there was a growing tension regarding the role of the Jews as God's chosen people. While this point was made very clear in the Hebrew Scriptures (the Old Testament), the early Church Fathers increasingly saw the Christians as having superseded the Jews, thus giving rise to what is today called Replacement Theology. This centres around the claim that the Church has replaced Israel as God's chosen people. This helped to lay the foundation for a radical anti-Judaic polemic, which in turn gave birth to centuries of anti-Semitism – but more on this later.

The teachings of Paul

The position of Paul is critical regarding the relationship between Jews and Christians. At certain points he is very proud of his own Jewish heritage and proud of the foundation of Judaism to his own faith. As mentioned, the main conflict appeared to be initially between the Jewish followers of Jesus and His Greek/Hellenistic followers. Did they or did they not need to follow all Judaic teaching? This became more of an issue as those who followed Jesus were increasingly from a Gentile background. The very first recorded church conflict was over Judaism.

The ministry of Jesus had very much been Israel-based and thus focused on the Jewish community. In essence it was a movement within observant Judaism, though it challenged many aspects of Pharisaic Judaism, which was the mainstream Orthodox Judaism of the day.

Paul taught that once a person had been baptized into the Christian faith, that was enough. He did not consider it necessary for non-Jewish followers of Jesus to observe Judaic law. But the other main leaders of the new faith tradition, Peter and James, considered the observance of Judaism to be more important. Both were former disciples of Jesus. James, the brother of Jesus, was regarded as the first Bishop of Jerusalem, while Peter was viewed as the very foundation upon which the Church was built.

Paul established his base in Antioch in Syria among a group of followers of the new faith tradition, and it was here that believers were first called *Christianoi* (in Greek) – the followers of Christ. At this time Paul was spearheading this part of the movement with Barnabas, while Peter and James remained based in Jerusalem, and their followers of Jesus were called the Nazarenes. Paul and Barnabas, aware of the growing separation between their two groups, went to Jerusalem for a serious conversation (which is outlined in Galatians chapter 2). Paul was very clear in his argument to Peter that observance of the Judaic law was not a means of or to salvation. It was not a replacement for the salvation that Jesus won by His death on the cross. In both Acts and Galatians we see portrayed the differences between these two groups of early Christians. These tensions laid the foundation for so much that was to come.

The Church Fathers

While in the biblical era we see a real tension existing between established Judaism and developing Christianity, what was to follow was so much more extreme. From the biblical era we move to the period of the Church Fathers – in reality, the first bishops of the Church. What they began to say about the Jews was often extremely inflammatory.

The greatest of the Church Fathers are revered to this day and include people such as St Augustine. He regarded himself as benevolent towards the Jews by stating that they should not be killed, but be left alive in a suffering state as a perpetual reminder that it was they who had murdered Christ. Thus they would continually remind the Church that they were in fact guilty of deicide, which is the killing of God. Many of the other Church Fathers, such as John Chrysostom, were even more extreme in their condemnation of the Jews. Here is a summary of what a few of the Church Fathers had to say about the Jews:

Ignatius of Antioch (c. AD 50–117)

Ignatius said that those who shared in the Passover were partaking with those responsible for killing Jesus, despite the Lord God declaring that the Passover was to be a feast forever.

Justin Martyr (AD 100–165)

Justin stated that God's covenant with Israel had ceased to be valid and that Gentile followers of Jesus had replaced the Jews as the people of God.

Irenaeus (c. AD 130–202)

Irenaeus made clear that the Jews were disinherited from the love of God.

Tertullian (c. AD 155–230)

Tertullian pronounced that since the Jews were responsible for the death of Jesus, they had been totally rejected by God.

Origen (AD 185–254)

Origen also stated that the Jews were responsible for the killing of Jesus. His influence was huge and thus he is seen as being responsible for much of the developing anti-Judaic polemic.

Eusebius (c. AD 275–339)

Eusebius argued that the biblical promises were meant for the Gentile followers of Jesus and that the curses were meant for the Jews. Thus, he said, the Church was now the true Israel and therefore the beneficiary of all the promises to Israel.

John Chrysostom (AD 349–407)

John Chrysostom is considered to be one of the great Church Fathers. He taught against the Jews, stating that their synagogues were no more than brothels and theatres; that they were frequented by thieves and were the place of wild beasts. He pictured the Jews as the worshippers of Satan, a demon-possessed people who could never be forgiven. It was therefore the Christian responsibility to hate all Jews.

Jerome (c. AD 347–420)

Jerome spoke of Jews as serpents who wore the image of Judas. Their psalms and prayers were seen as nothing more than the sounds of braying donkeys and they had a total inability to understand Scripture.

Ephraim the Syrian (AD 306–373)

Ephraim, who is much revered here in the Middle East, continually wrote treatises and even poems against the Jews. He saw them as a satanic people who actively worked with Satan in order to deceive Christians and get them to return to Judaism. He presented the Jews as not only the profound opponents of Christianity, but those who were literally the overt enemies of Christianity. Christianity was seen as the religion of the Almighty, which was all about peace, while Judaism was not only a totally false religion, but totally satanic. He saw his job as doing everything in his power to prevent the new Christians from returning to Judaism.

What is particularly difficult, from my position as a church leader, is that so many of these Church Fathers were profound leaders of the early Christian faith. If one were not aware of their radical anti-Judaic polemic, one would see them as deeply holy figures. These men were not seen as an ancient form of the Klu Klux Klan, but as devout, holy, religious leaders.

Here, at the very beginning of Christianity, we see the foundations laid for what would become radical anti-Semitism. What is more, it was given total theological justification. As one studies the issue, it is perfectly obvious that everything that happened was totally and utterly opposed to the teachings of Jesus.

The early church councils
The early church councils also made clear statements against the Jews.

The Council of Elvira (AD 305 in Spain)
This council prohibited Christians from marrying Jews, observing the Sabbath with them or even eating a meal with them.

The Council of Nicaea (AD 325 in Turkey)
The Council of Nicaea is seen as one of the main historic and foundational meetings of the Church. It was the council that established the foundation of the creed used by much of the Church to this day. While laying the doctrinal foundation of the Church, this council also worked to disassociate Easter from the Passover. Their argument was that the celebration of Easter should have nothing to do with the Jewish festival, since the Jews were evil.

The Middle Ages
By the Middle Ages the anti-Judaic polemic was so rooted in Christianity that it was almost considered Christian doctrine. At the very heart of Christian belief was the fact that the Jews were Christ-killers and thus guilty of deicide, the worst crime imaginable. There was no church that spoke in defence of the Jews. The widely held Christian position was even popularized in the passion plays, which just reiterated the idea of the Jews as the killers of Jesus. They presented the Jews as demonic-looking figures whose intent was simply to try to kill Christians. There was also the popular belief

that Jews would steal communion wafers and then stab them with a dagger, thus killing Jesus again. Then belief in "blood libels" developed. These were the widespread rumours that each year at Passover, Jews would kill Christians, especially children, to use their blood to share in satanic rituals.

This was the time of the crusades and inquisitions. The Middle Ages were also the years of the Black Death. Millions of people died, but very few Jews succumbed. Rumours spread that Jews were poisoning the Christians' wells. The fact that so few Jews died was clearly because of Jewish Kashrut (dietary laws) and the observance of the strict sanitary rules and conditions laid down in the Hebrew Scriptures. But Christians began attacking Jews in fear and anger. The result was that some Jewish communities were totally destroyed and many Jews were burnt to death or tortured.

At the time, the second city of England was Norwich. It had a considerable Jewish population, most of whom had moved there from London. At first, the Jews of Norwich lived a good life, as their excellent records prove. Things clearly changed for the Jews there after the death of a child known as William of Norwich, who later became known as St William.

William was a boy of just eleven or twelve who was found dead in woods near to the town on 24 March 1144. Stories developed that he was taken by the Jews, killed and bound to a cross with his head shaved. The fact that it happened close to Passover added credence to the story that Jews were killing children so that their blood could be used in sacrificial acts. The stories about William increased. Though never canonized by the pope, he was revered as a saint who was killed for his faith. Eventually his remains were buried at Norwich Cathedral. With the death of William the blood libels began. Around the country it was not long before there were many accusations being made against the Jews, thus justifying their murder in retribution.

Throughout Europe the torture and murder of the Jews continued. Then came the Spanish Inquisition, when Pope Sixtus IV granted a special agreement to King Ferdinand and Queen Isabella of Spain. They were permitted to conduct an inquisition against all baptized Jews who maintained Jewish practices. This agreement literally sanctioned the slaughter of thousands of Jews and resulted in the expulsion of over 150,000 Jews from Spain.

In the next chapter, I will examine the impact of the Reformation on Central European attitudes towards the Jewish people.

The Rift Continues: Jews and Christians

The Reformation

The Reformation brought with it a great many positive changes to the Church, but one problem it did not fix was the hatred towards the Jewish people. Martin Luther, the leader of the Reformation, had a short-lived positive attitude towards the Jews. At first he taught that they had rejected the gospel because of the intense corruption in the Roman Catholic Church. When the Jews failed to follow his Reformation, however, he developed a very clear polemic against them. In 1543 he published what is still seen today as one of the worst anti-Judaic publications, entitled *On the Jews and Their Lies*.

In today's world, such a publication would be seen as

vehemently anti-Semitic, yet it originated from one of the most respected Christian leaders of all time. In it he referred to the Jews as "miserable, blind and senseless" and "thieves and robbers, blind and venomous".

Luther did not stop there. He continued with his assessment of what should happen to the Jews. He presented a diatribe that assured me, as a theological student and a Christian, that I should dedicate my life to Jewish–Christian relations and facilitate reconciliation wherever possible. Here is Luther's list of things that he believed should happen to the Jews:

1. Their synagogues and schools should be burnt.
2. Their houses should be destroyed.
3. Their Talmudic writings should be confiscated.
4. Their rabbis should be forbidden to teach.
5. Their money should be taken from them.
6. They should be compelled to do forced labour.

The division continues

Many prominent scholars agree that Luther's treatise had a major influence on Central European attitudes towards Jews in the period leading up to the Second World War and the Holocaust, known in Hebrew as the *Shoa*. Four hundred years after it was written, Nazis had copies of Luther's book on display at the Nuremberg rallies. Adolf Hitler, in his book *Mein Kampf*, referred to Luther as not only a great reformer, but also a great "warrior and a true statesman". In other words, he drew upon Luther's writings to justify his own radical brand of anti-Semitism. It is important to point out that many Lutheran church bodies have denounced Luther's teaching regarding the Jews and disassociated themselves from it. But it is tragic that such beliefs should be incubated in the heart of Christian Europe. The anti-Judaic polemic was widespread among both the Roman Catholic and the Protestant churches. Even during the post-war Nuremberg trials, there were defendants who justified their actions with the words of Luther.

Many Christians do not accept these terrible facts, but I believe that they are an inerasable part of the Church's history. How did the Church stray so far from the teachings of Jesus? I am brought back to Temple's words, "When religion goes wrong, it goes very wrong."

The expulsion of the Jews from the UK and their subsequent return

There had been a very small Jewish population in the UK as far back as Roman times. But it was only in 1066 that William the Conqueror first encouraged Jews from France to come and settle in England. Jews came thinking that they were escaping anti-Semitism, but sadly, it followed them. There were attacks upon various Jews who had taken residence in major cities such as Norwich, London and York. The year 1144 saw the first blood libel charge, as outlined in the previous chapter, when the Jews of Norwich were charged with killing a child to use his blood for Passover. Such charges were then repeated throughout various cities in England.

In March 1190, while Richard I was away fighting in the crusades, various riots against the Jews broke out in England. The worst of these took place in York. A large number of people there had become envious of the wealth of the Jews, and many Jewish homes were destroyed. Out of desperation, many Jews took refuge in the Clifford's Towers. Cut off and without food, many of them killed themselves. On 16 March the castle was captured and those who were still alive were slaughtered. This was the worst massacre in the history of the Jews in Britain.

The Jews in England continued to have a difficult life, with much opposition. When Edward I became king, the identification of Jews became compulsory. Every Jew above the age of seven was required to wear a yellow badge. The Yellow Star of David started not in Germany under Hitler, but in England under a Christian king.

It was in 1255, in Lincoln, that a major development concerning the anti-Judaic polemic in England took place – an incident similar to that of William of Norwich. A young boy called Hugh was chasing a ball when he fell down a well. This well happened to belong to a Jewish family. Hugh was found dead a few weeks later. Because Jews owned the well, there were accusations that they had killed him. The result was more blood libel charges and attacks against the Jews, with over 100 being executed. The Jews declared that they would leave the city, but Henry III did not allow this. He saw the Jews as his property to control.

In 1290 Edward I became the first monarch to expel all Jews from a European nation. Most Jews fled to France or Germany, and a few to Holland. England was therefore devoid of a Jewish presence for 350 years until the era of Oliver Cromwell.

During the 350 years when the Jews were absent from England, a huge amount happened, not least the English Reformation and the Civil War, which led to the removal and murder of Charles I. Ultimate power was now placed in the hands of Oliver Cromwell, who took the title of Lord Protector.

Cromwell was, in essence, king, president and prime minister all in one. He held total power as the sole leader of the country. The Civil War that brought him to power was essentially about the struggle between Catholics and the newly formed Protestant Church as well as between the monarchy and Parliament. Charles I refused to put his Catholic inheritance behind him while Parliament was, on the whole, following a Protestant tradition.

The Protestant Church was totally opposed to what it believed was the non-biblical (and to them, non-Christian) stance of the Catholic Church. The Protestants rejected many of the Vatican's teachings, including those about purgatory and especially the indulgences sold by the Holy See (the episcopal jurisdiction of the Catholic

Church in Rome), supposedly to prevent people from having to endure purgatory.

As a part of this reformed theology, Cromwell's people began to express concern over interpretation of the Holy Bible. While they had a considerable understanding of the *Koine* Greek of the New Testament, there was a total lack of understanding of Hebrew. This situation was made worse by the fact that there were no Jews in England.

It was therefore decided that senior ministers of the Church of England should learn Hebrew to enable them to ensure that theirs was a proper translation of the Hebrew Scriptures. Since they could no longer learn Hebrew in England, it was decided that they should go to the Netherlands to study under the rabbis there.

The Jewish community in the Netherlands was one of the most significant in Europe. Despite the Netherlands being in the heart of Western Europe (which, in Jewish terms, meant that they were *Ashkenazi*), most of the Jews of the Netherlands were actually *Sephardi* (i.e. coming from Spain and Portugal), so in essence they were oriental. There were also *Marranos* in the Netherlands. These were Jews who had accepted Christianity and had been baptized, but were often still practising Jewish customs.

As you read the history of the Jews in the Netherlands, you need to be aware that millenarianism (the belief in the imminent return of the Lord resulting in the establishment of a 1,000-year messianic reign on Earth) was becoming increasingly significant among people who saw themselves as a product of the Reformation. This was precisely the position that was being held by Cromwell and many of his followers.

The act of Cromwell in sending some of his ministers to the Netherlands was partly due to the fact that he had developed a unique relationship with the famous Dutch rabbi, Manesseh Ben Israel. He and his people profoundly influenced the English ministers while they were learning Hebrew. The issue of the observance of Scripture became increasingly important to them. They also began to understand more about the theology of covenant. God was faithful to His people, the Jews, forever. The Christians were also in everlasting covenant with God. In this way the Christians began to see themselves as intrinsically connected to the Jews, since they both shared in the covenant. This was not an early form of Replacement Theology, but the beginning of what is now called Christian Zionism – a theology that has at its heart God's eternal faithfulness to His people, the Jews.

It is interesting to consider the history regarding what led to the Jews being allowed to return to England in 1657. Much has been written about the need, at the time, for inward investment to improve the economic foundation of England after the Civil War. Very few people mention the major theological dimensions that profoundly influenced Cromwell's decision to allow the Jews to return to England.

He hosted what was called the Whitehall Conference with the sole aim of discussing the return of the Jews to England. Once again, the divide was between those who saw it purely as a political and economic issue and those who saw it as a profoundly religious issue.

Cromwell argued eloquently from a biblical viewpoint. For him, the main issue was that the Jews were the people of God, and this fact was intrinsically linked to how followers of Jesus should treat God's everlasting people. In the Barebones Parliament (also known as the Little Parliament, the Nominated Assembly and the Parliament of Saints), which came into being on 4 July 1653, Cromwell declared:

> Indeed, I do think something is at the door: we are at the threshold... you are at the edge of the promises and prophecies... it may be, as some think, God will bring the Jews home to their station "from the isles of the sea" and answer their expectations "as from the depths of the sea"... Truly you are called by God, "as Judah was" to "rule with him" and for him.

Cromwell saw that the way in which Christians had treated Jews historically was a profound reason for the Reformation and the breaking from the Roman Catholic Church. He did not hold to the anti-Judaic polemic that had been continued by people such as Luther.

The rabbi from Holland, Manasseh Ben Israel, was a prolific author, and he dedicated one of his books to Cromwell and the British Government before the Jews were allowed back into England. This was *The Hope of Israel*, written in 1652. Then, in 1655, he wrote *Vindiciae Judaeorum* (*The Vindication of the Jews*), which attempted to answer some of the questions proposed by some of the senior Puritans (those who held strongly to Protestant views and who had become the political leaders with Cromwell as well as the leaders of the Reformed church).

The return of the Jews to England was much sought after by many of the Dutch Jews, and Rabbi Manasseh Ben Israel was an integral part of the movement seeking their return. What was so interesting was that the Jews and the Christian millenarian followers had much in common with each other. In essence, what was happening was very different to anything that had happened before: Christians were becoming more aligned with Jewish thought, practice and understanding.

One example of this related to the issue of the commandment to keep the Sabbath holy. The Sabbath clearly means the sixth day of the week. Some Christians were beginning to say, "Are not the Ten Commandments forever? How can we justify keeping nine and not ten?" So many began to observe the Sabbath. They may have worshipped in church on Sunday, but Saturday became a day of rest.

So Jews were allowed to return to England and were granted most of the rights of all British citizens. They were also allowed to build synagogues – one of the first being the Bevis Marks Sephardi Synagogue in the City of London, to this day the foremost Sephardi synagogue in the United Kingdom. Many of its early members were the same Sephardi Jews who came via Holland. They were also allowed to establish Jewish cemeteries, which were of great importance to this ancient spiritual tradition.

Despite much debate, it cannot be denied that at the very heart of the Jews' return to England was Cromwell's submission of his seven-point petition to the Council of State on 31 October 1655, calling for their return. Also, a crucial role was played by Manasseh Ben Israel, who became known as "the Ambassador to the Gentiles".

The return of the Jews to England started a new era of freedom for them there. In Europe, relations with the Jewish people continued to be erratic. Periods of freedom were followed by periods of great adversity and the development of pogroms (strategic mass attacks) with the aim of segregating Jews from the masses. This anti-Jewish activity continued to be supported by various churches.

In the Middle East, now under Islamic control, relations with the Jews continued to be very diverse. At times, in places such as Iraq, Jews were given much freedom and played a very prominent role in society.

Here Jews and Christians both lived as *dhimmi* – a special status under Islamic law for non-Muslim citizens of an Islamic state. *Dhimmis* were "people of the Book" (the "Book" being the Bible) who occupied a role of servitude and had to pay a special tax (the *Jizyah*) to the Islamic authorities. This tax was levied on non-Islamic communities and was applied equally to both Jews and Christians. Finally, they both had something in common in the Middle East!

The pendulum swings

The generally positive attitude towards Jews in Britain remained, but the theological similarities with those under Cromwell – such as the concentration of the Jews in Christendom along with its accompanying millenarianism – soon disappeared. Things continued in a similar vein for the next 200 years in Europe, with increasingly frequent pogroms and regular anti-Judaic aggression. Christian millenarianism did not surface again in Britain until the 1850s with the rise of the Holiness Movement, which brought with it an increased concern for Judaism and even the return of the Jews to Israel.

This concern was prevalent in two further movements that developed during this era. Many people became part of the Unitarian movement, stressing that God was One, and were thus opposed to mainstream Trinitarians. Among this group were some very significant people, such as the prominent politician Joseph Chamberlain, one time chancellor of the exchequer and later foreign minister. The second movement that developed, which was strictly Trinitarian, was the Brethren movement.

It is interesting to see how many politicians were influenced by both of these, not only those who held to either denominational position. One such person was the foreign secretary Arthur James Balfour, who wrote a short letter (known as the Balfour Declaration of 1926) to Baron Rothschild, a leader of the British Jewish community, stating the Government's intention to work for the establishment of a homeland for the Jewish people.

The period at the end of the nineteenth century saw the radical growth of serious pro-Jewish and pro-Zionist movements within the Church. Many of the issues that surfaced in the time of Oliver Cromwell again came to the fore, predominantly the belief that God was still involved with, and concerned for, the Jewish people. Many books were written in this period justifying this position, notably *Israel My Glory* (John Wilkinson, 1890), *The Jewish Problem – Its Solution or Israel's Present and Future* (David Baron, 1891) and *The Ancient Scriptures and the Modern Jew* (David Baron, 1900).

As David Baron's titles suggest, there was a new millenarianism. Just as there had been in Cromwell's era, there was a new concentration on the role of the Jews even before the Balfour Declaration.

The Holocaust (or *Shoa*)

The name of the worst tragedy in history is itself controversial. The term "holocaust" is Greek in origin, coming from the word that is used to describe pagan sacrificial burnings. Many in the Jewish community, especially in Israel, have objected to this very term. In Hebrew the term used is *Shoa*, which simply means "the catastrophe".

While it cannot be said that a Christian anti-Judaic polemic was a direct cause of the Holocaust, the fact remains that it happened in the midst of a so-called Christian Europe. Furthermore, it could not have happened unless it had been incubated in an environment where the foundations for such an evil atrocity had been laid. The theology of the Church for nearly 2,000 years had helped to create a culture in which an evil man such as Hitler could justify murdering 6 million Jewish people.

The following figures compiled by Lucy Dawidowicz, published in her *The War Against the Jews: 1933–1945*, give a fairly precise list of where the victims came from and how many were killed. She was an amazing American Jewish historian who did a lot of significant work with the Jews in Europe, both before and after the Holocaust. Her research clearly shows the horrendous fact that 67 per cent of all the Jews in Europe were killed.

Country	Est. pre-war Jewish pop	Est. killed	% killed
Poland	3,300,000	3,000,000	90%
Baltic States	253,000	228,000	90%
Germany & Austria	240,000	210,000	90%
Bohemia & Moravia	90,000	80,000	89%
Slovakia	90,000	75,000	83%
Greece	70,000	54,000	77%
Netherlands	140,000	105,000	75%
Hungary	650,000	450,000	70%
Belorus	375,000	245,000	65%
Ukraine	1,500,000	900,000	60%
Belgium	65,000	40,000	60%
Yugoslavia	43,000	26,000	60%
Romania	600,000	300,000	50%
Norway	1,800	900	50%
France	350,000	90,000	26%
Bulgaria	64,000	14,000	22%
Italy	40,000	8,000	20%
Luxembourg	5,000	1,000	20%
Russia	975,000	107,000	11%
Finland	2,000	–	–
Denmark	8,000	–	–
Total	**8,861,800**	**5,933,900**	**67%**

While much of this happened during the Second World War, the British Prime Minister at the time was none other than the son of the great pro-Jewish Unitarian politician Joseph Chamberlain, the not-so-great Neville Chamberlain, the man who came back from seeing Hitler waving a piece of paper saying, "Peace in our time."

During the war Britain had an outstanding Archbishop of Canterbury in William Temple. He was so distressed when he heard the news of the Holocaust that he helped establish the Council of Christians and Jews in 1942 with the chief rabbi Joseph Herzel. It was not until after the Second World War, though, that the severity of the tragedy became fully known. After the war Christian leaders had to think seriously about how this had happened.

The International Council of Christians and Jews was established, with Christians from many countries, especially in Europe, asking how something as evil as the Holocaust could happen in their midst. The remaining Jews and Christians started to work together. An emergency meeting was held in 1947 in Seelisberg in which the Christian leaders asked fundamental questions about what had happened to Christian theology and Christian thought. They came up with ten points, which showed how Christian theology needed to radically change.

The Ten Points of Seelisberg

The following statement, produced by the Christian participants at the second conference of the newly formed International Council of Christians and Jews (ICCJ), was made as Christians began to come to terms with the implications of the Holocaust:

1. Remember that One God speaks to us all through the Old and the New Testaments.

2. Remember that Jesus was born of a Jewish mother of the seed of David and the people of Israel, and that His everlasting love and forgiveness embraces His own people and the whole world.

3. Remember that the first disciples, the apostles and the first martyrs were Jews.

4. Remember that the fundamental commandment of Christianity, to love God and one's neighbour, proclaimed already in the Old Testament and confirmed by Jesus, is binding upon both Christians and Jews in all human relationships, without any exception.

5. Avoid distorting or misrepresenting biblical or post-biblical Judaism with the object of extolling Christianity.

6. Avoid using the word "Jews" in the exclusive sense of the enemies of Jesus and the words "The Enemies of Jesus" to designate the whole Jewish people.

7. Avoid presenting the Passion in such a way as to bring the odium of the killing of Jesus upon all Jews or upon Jews alone. It was only a section of the Jews in Jerusalem who demanded the death of Jesus, and the Christian message has always been that it was the sins

of mankind which were exemplified by those Jews and the sins in which all men share that brought Christ to the Cross.

8. Avoid referring to the scriptural curses, or the cry of a raging mob: "His Blood be Upon Us and Our Children", without remembering that this cry should not count against the infinitely more weighty words of our Lord: "Father, Forgive Them, for They Know not What They Do."

9. Avoid promoting the superstitious notion that the Jewish people are reprobate, accursed, reserved for a destiny of suffering.

10. Avoid speaking of the Jews as if the first members of the Church had not been Jews.

Here, for the first time, was a serious assessment of what was wrong with Christian theology. For nearly 2,000 years it had both supported and even created an anti-Judaic message. From its very beginning Christianity had not only created an anti-Judaic polemic, but had denied so many of the essential components of the Christian faith. It had been far from what Jesus the Jew had intended for His followers.

For over sixty years the Seelisberg document of the ICCJ remained the most significant document on the issue of the relationship between Jews and Christians. Then, in 2008, the ICCJ called another major conference in Berlin to update the statement, written in the light of the *Shoa*. This later statement was longer and went into more depth than Seelisberg. It was called "A Time for Recommitment" and reads as follows:

A Time for Recommitment

We commit ourselves to the following goals and invite all Christians and Christian communities to join us in the continuing effort to remove all vestiges of contempt towards Jews and enhance bonds with the Jewish communities worldwide.

1. To combat religious, racial and all other forms of anti-Semitism

Biblically

- By recognising Paul's profound identity as a Jew of his day, and interpreting his writings within the contextual framework of first-century Judaism.

- By emphasising that recent scholarship on both the commonality and gradual separation of Christianity and Judaism is critical for our basic understanding of the Jewish–Christian relationship.

- By presenting the two Testaments in the Christian Bible as complementary and mutually affirming rather than antagonistic or inferior/superior.

Denominations that use lectionaries are encouraged to choose and link biblical texts that offer such an affirming theology.

- By speaking out against Christian misreadings of biblical texts regarding Jews and Judaism that can provoke caricatures or animosity.

Liturgically

- By highlighting the connection between Jewish and Christian liturgy.

- By drawing upon the spiritual richness of Jewish interpretations of the scriptures.

- By cleansing Christian liturgies of anti-Jewish perspectives, particularly in preaching, prayers and hymns.

Catechetically

- By presenting the Christian–Jewish relationship in positive tones in the education of Christians of all ages, underlining the Jewish foundations of Christian belief and accurately describing the ways Jews themselves understand their own traditions and practices. This includes the curricula of Christian schools, seminaries and adult education programs.

- By promoting awareness of the long-lived traditions of Christian anti-Judaism and providing models for renewing the unique Jewish–Christian relationship.

- By underscoring the immense religious wealth found in the Jewish tradition, especially by studying its authoritative texts.

2. To promote interreligious dialogue with Jews

- By understanding dialogue as requiring trust and equality among all participants and rejecting any notion of convincing others to accept one's own beliefs.

- By appreciating that dialogue encourages participants to examine critically their own perceptions of both their own tradition and that of their dialogue partners in the light of a genuine engagement with the other.

3. To develop theological understandings of Judaism that affirm its distinctive integrity

- By eliminating any teachings that Christians have replaced Jews as a people in covenant with God.

- By emphasising the common mission of Jews and Christians in preparing the world for the kingdom of God or the Age to Come.

- By establishing equal, reciprocal working relationships with Jewish religious and civic organisations.

- By ensuring that emerging theological movements from Asia, Africa and Latin America, and feminist, liberationist or other approaches integrate an accurate understanding of Judaism and Christian–Jewish relations into their theological formulations.

- By opposing organised efforts at the conversion of Jews.

4. To pray for the peace of Jerusalem

- By promoting the belief in an inherent connectedness between Christians and Jews.

- By understanding more fully Judaism's deep attachment to the Land of Israel as a fundamental religious perspective and many Jewish people's connection with the State of Israel as a matter of physical and cultural survival.

- By reflecting on ways that the Bible's spiritual understanding of the land can be better incorporated into Christian faith perspectives.

- By critiquing the policies of Israeli and Palestinian governmental and social institutions when such criticism is morally warranted, at the same time acknowledging both communities' deep attachment to the land.

- By critiquing attacks on Zionism particularly when they become expressions of anti-Semitism.

- By joining with Jewish, Christian and Muslim peace workers, with Israelis and Palestinians, to build trust and peace in a Middle East where all can live secure in independent, viable states rooted in international law and guaranteed human rights.

- By enhancing the security and prosperity of Christian communities both in Israel and Palestine.

- By working for improved relations among Jews, Christians and Muslims in the Middle East and the rest of the world.

A Call To Jews and Jewish Communities

We commit ourselves to the following goals and invite all Jews and Jewish communities to join us in the continuing effort to remove all vestiges of animosity and caricature toward Christians and to enhance bonds with Christian churches of the world.

5. To acknowledge the efforts of many Christian communities in the late 20th century to reform their attitudes toward Jews

- By learning about these reforms through more intensive dialogue with Christians.

- By discussing the implications of changes in Christian churches regarding Jews and their understandings of Judaism.

- By teaching Jews of all ages about these changes, both in the context of the history of Jewish–Christian relations and according to the appropriate stage of education for each group.

- By including basic and accurate background information about Christianity in the curricula of Jewish schools, rabbinic seminaries and adult education programs.

- By studying the New Testament both as Christianity's sacred text and as literature written to a large degree by Jews in an historical–cultural context similar to early Rabbinic literature, thereby offering insight into the development of Judaism in the early centuries of the Common Era.

6. To re-examine Jewish texts and liturgy in the light of these Christian reforms

- By grappling with Jewish texts that appear xenophobic or racist, realising that many religious traditions have uplifting, inspirational texts as well as problematic ones. The emphasis for all religious traditions should be on texts that promote tolerance and openness.

- By placing problematic texts within their historical context, in particular writings from the times when Jews were a powerless, persecuted and humiliated minority.

- By addressing the possible re-interpretation, change or omission of parts of Jewish liturgy that treat others in problematic ways.

7. To differentiate between fair-minded criticism of Israel and anti-Semitism

- By understanding and promoting biblical examples of just criticism as expressions of loyalty and love.

- By helping Christians appreciate that communal identity and interconnectedness are intrinsic to Jewish self-understanding, in addition to religious faith and practice, therefore making the commitment to the survival and security of the State of Israel of great importance to most Jews.

8. To offer encouragement to the State of Israel as it works to fulfil the ideals stated in its founding documents, a task Israel shares with many nations of the world.

- By ensuring equal rights for religious and ethnic minorities, including Christians, living within the Jewish state.

- By achieving a just and peaceful resolution of the Israeli–Palestinian conflict.

A Call To Both Christian and Jewish Communities and Others

We commit ourselves to the following goals and invite Jews, Christians and Muslims, together with all people of faith and goodwill, always to respect the other and to accept each other's differences and dignity.

9. To enhance interreligious and intercultural education

- By combating negative images of others, teaching the foundational truth that each human being is created in the image of God.

1. The Iraqi delegation in Coventry Cathedral on their first visit to England in 1999. Standing in front of the sanctuary ruins which say, "Father, forgive", are (left to right): Grand Ayatollah Hussein Al Sadr; Father Philip; the late Chaldean patriarch Raphael Bidawid I; Sheikh Abdul Latif Humayem (the Sunni leader and former imam to Saddam Hussein); and Canon White.

2. At the home of Grand Ayatollah Hussein Al Sadr in 2010. Left to right: St George's curate; Father Faiz; Canon White; the Grand Ayatollah; Bishop Michael Lewis; and the then FRRME director, Peter Marsden.

3. Senior Shia, Sunni, and Christian leaders meet in Copenhagen in January 2011 to discuss how reconciliation can be taken forward.

1

2

3

4

5

6

4. Sunni, Shia, and Christian religious leaders meet in September 2012 at St George's Church with the archdeacon, the Venerable Canon Bill Schwartz (fourth from left).

5. Sheikh Khalid Al Mullah and Sayed Jawad Al Khoi receiving the 2012 FRRME Peace Prize in front of the Queen's throne in the House of Lords. From left to right: Alistair Burt, Middle East Foreign Secretary; Lord Hylton, Chairman of the Foundation Board; Canon White; Sheikh Khalid Al Mullah, Gehad Hanna, Sayed Jawad Al Khoi, and Lord George Carey, the patron of FRRME.

6. Two of Canon White's closest friends, Sheikh Khalid Al Mullah, the Sunni leader in Iraq, and Sayed Jawad Al Khoi, the young Shia leader of FRRME's work with the Rt Hon. Tony Blair and Canon White. They were in London to receive the 2012 FRRME Peace Prize.

7. From left to right: Sheikh Hafeed, one of the most significant Kurdish religious leaders; Sheikh Khalid Al Mullah, Yonadam Khanna, the most senior Christian politician in Iraq, with an interpreter, and Lord Hylton in the background. The group met in Beirut in 2010 to discuss how to enable forgiveness in order to prevent the pain of the past from determining the future.

8. Michael Manthei and Jason Westerfield, visiting American pastors, with the only Christian minister in Iraq, the Minister of Environment, Sargon Slewa, together with Canon White in 2012.

9. Canon White meeting (from left to right): Sheikh Mohammed; Sheikh Ahmed; Sheikh Khalid Al Mullah; and Paul White, FRRME's Middle East Project Officer, in 2012 in order to discuss future reconciliation meetings.

10. Sheikh Khalid Al Mullah and Canon White spend time together developing their friendship in 2012.

11. Shia, Sunni, and Christian leaders meet together and listen to each other's stories in 2012.

12. General George Sada, Canon White, and the current archbishop of Canterbury, Justin Welby, working on satellite phones outside Saddam Hussein's palace in 2003. The Republican Palace in Baghdad became the headquarters of the Coalition Provisional Authority.

13. The first service at the reopening of St George's Church in 2003. From left to right: the current archbishop of Canterbury, Justin Welby, Hanna the caretaker and his daughter Marriam, and Canon White.

14

14. Sheikh Khalif and Canon White stand in front of Ezekiel's tomb in 2011 in an ancient Jewish synagogue, which now functions as a mosque.

15. The present-day clinic at St George's Church, Baghdad. It offers real hope and healing to people of all faith traditions. There are doctors' offices, dental suites, a pharmacy, and a laboratory, as well as X-ray, haematology, and stem-cell therapy units.

15

16

16. *From left to right*: Amb. Emmanuel Thomi, Lord Hylton, and Canon White at a meeting with Grand Ayatollah Najafi, one of the most senior ayatollahs in Iraq, in October of 2011 at his residence in Najaf.

17. January 2002: The original signing of the Alexandria Declaration in which Jewish, Christian, and Muslim leaders committed themselves to work for peace in the Holy Land. It was chaired by the then archbishop of Canterbury, George Carey, and Grand Imam of Al Azhar, Sheikh Tantawi.

18. One of the ongoing meetings of the Alexandria Committee in Jerusalem in 2004, two years after the signing of the original declaration, at which the then archbishop of Canterbury, Rowan Williams, was present.

17

18

19. Meeting in Cairo with the Islamic leaders of Palestine in 2004. The Jewish leaders of Israel were also present at this meeting, but both groups were too afraid to be seen photographed together.

20. Further meetings and engagement of the permanent committee for the implementation of the Alexandria Declaration in 2004.

- By making the removal of prejudices against the other a high priority in the educational process.

- By encouraging mutual study of religious texts, so that Jews, Christians, Muslims and members of other religious groups can learn both from and with each other.

- By supporting common social action in the pursuit of common values.

10. To promote interreligious friendship and cooperation as well as social justice in the global society

- By rejoicing in the uniqueness of each person, and promoting everyone's political, economic and social well-being.

- By recognising as equal citizens members of faith traditions who have migrated to new homelands where they may have become part of a religious minority.

- By striving for equal rights for all people, regardless of their religion, gender or sexual orientation.

- By recognising and grappling with the fact that feelings of religious superiority – and an accompanying sense that other religions are inferior – are present in each tradition, including one's own.

11. To enhance dialogue with political and economic bodies

- By collaborating with political and economic bodies whenever possible to promote interreligious understanding.

- By benefiting from political and economic groups' growing interest in interreligious relations.

- By initiating discussion with political and economic bodies around the urgent need for justice in the global community.

12. To network with all those whose work responds to the demands of environmental stewardship

- By fostering commitment to the belief that every human being is entrusted with the care of the Earth.

- By recognising the shared Jewish and Christian biblical duty toward creation, and the responsibility to bring it to bear in public discourse and action.

This document deals with many of the issues which then faced and still face Jews and Christians. Two very important issues were mentioned: one being the relationship with Islam and the other being the establishment of the State of Israel. It is a truly amazing document but, sadly, not one that all churches follow.

While the statement was accepted by many academics and those concerned with Jewish relations, many other Christians have seen the Israeli–Palestinian crisis as a means to attack the Jewish community.

We cannot look at one part of the world and say it was exempt from the terrors of anti-Judaism. As we have seen in the previous sections, Britain did not participate in perpetrating the *Shoa*, but it did have an anti-Judaic history. This did not automatically change after the war, either. Many of the few who survived the horrors of the death camps tried to make their way to Israel/Palestine – their hoped-for Promised Land. But the land was under British control at that time, and many of those who arrived on its shores were physically removed to Cyprus. In Cyprus, also under British control, they were put into other "camps". They had survived the death camps, yet many actually died in *these* camps, owned by the British. This is yet another thing that reminds us that nobody was innocent of anti-Judaic polemic.

The re-establishment of the State of Israel in 1948

For nearly 2,000 years the Jews had been without a homeland. After the catastrophe of the *Shoa* the future of the Jews had to be taken seriously. The issue was discussed at the League of Nations, the precursor of the United Nations. To the surprise of many, Israel was reborn, but this was also the beginning of new problems.

As soon as the state was established, the 1948 Arab–Israeli war (the war of independence) began. While there was much rejoicing by some over the rebirth of Israel, it signalled a new chapter of suffering for the Palestinian Arabs of the land. Many of them lost their land and homes. Many became refugees in Lebanon and Jordan, including many indigenous Christians. Now began a new problem in the Christian relationship with the Jews. But before we continue with this issue, it is essential that we recap on and summarize the theologies we have already seen.

CHAPTER 6

The Three Christian Theological Views

The Christian theologies towards the Jews can be broken down into what I call "the Three R's": Replacement Theology, Remnant Theology and Recognition Theology.

Replacement Theology

In essence, this theological viewpoint has at its core the belief that the Church has now "replaced" the Jews and Israel as God's "special" people. In other words, everything that applied historically and biblically to the Jewish nation now applies to the Church. Yet it was this belief, still perpetuated today, that gave rise to the radical anti-Judaic polemic, since according to its tenets the Jews and Israel were redundant in God's plans. From the very beginnings of Christianity, this theology held the view that the Jews, as a whole, were guilty of deicide; being responsible for the death of Jesus. Continuing through the Church Fathers and on to the Reformation and beyond, it has been responsible for the terrible history outlined in the previous chapter. It cannot be denied that this anti-Semitic theology engendered an atmosphere in Europe where the Holocaust/*Shoa* could happen. At the Nuremberg trials some of the greatest perpetrators of this atrocity said that they had only done what their great reformer Martin Luther had told them to do.

The establishment of the State of Israel only made things worse. Soon Replacement Theology became linked to the plight of the Palestinians, especially Palestinian Christians. The plight of persecuted Christians became an increasing issue to many established international church networks. Yet the Church was divided, as different factions were seen to hold to different positions. Some were pro-Palestine while others were pro-Israel. Even within church factions, opinions were often divided. This is still particularly so in the Church of England, which is divided between those who are seen to be supporting either Israel or Palestine. The normal split in the Church between evangelicals and liberals does not apply here; in this scenario it is far more complex.

Liberation Theology

As an aside, in recent years one of the offshoots of Replacement Theology has been Liberation Theology. This originated in South America and is a theological viewpoint that leans towards the oppressed. In essence, it expresses the view that God must always be on the side of those who are either poor or oppressed. It did not take long before a Palestinian Anglican churchman, Canon Naim Ateek, developed what he called a Palestinian Theology of Liberation. God was seen as favouring the oppressed people, in this case the Palestinians. Part and parcel of this theology was an avoidance of anything in the Bible that could be seen as being pro-Israel. Even major parts of the Bible, central to Christian as well as Jewish liturgy, such as the psalms, were seen as being too one-sided to be used.

This radical theology has seriously impacted the tourist industry, with many companies aligning themselves totally with this stance. Canon Ateek established the Sabeel Centre in Jerusalem, which a huge number of pilgrims now visit. Many returning from their pilgrimages say that they must work for peace in Israel/Palestine by supporting the work of this centre. One of the things that people fail to realize is that whoever you listen to in Israel or Palestine will present a compelling and totally convincing argument for their side. Plus, visitors to this centre are usually accommodated in Palestinian hotels in East Jerusalem, which limits their encounter with the reality of the land.

The influence of those who hold to this position is very serious, not least in the councils of various church denominations. From the Presbyterian Church in the USA to the Church of England's General Synod, some vehemently anti-Israel/anti-Judaic statements have been made. They have called for people not to purchase any Israeli products, especially those produced by Israeli Jews in Judea and Samaria (the West Bank).

The fact is, not all Israelis are Jews – there are many Muslim and Christian Israelis too. Many Jews regard the Palestinian Theology of Liberation as blatant anti-Semitism. The sad fact is, it is just another form of Replacement Theology under a new name, and it results in the same radical anti-Judaic polemic as before.

Supersessionism

Another form of Replacement Theology is Supersessionism or Fulfilment Theology. Central to this position is the belief that the New Covenant has replaced the Mosaic or Old Covenant. Therefore, the Christian Church is viewed as the inheritor of God's promises to Israel – the everlasting Old Covenant with the people of Israel somehow being replaced by a New Covenant with Christianity.

In essence, Supersessionism is the claim that God's covenant with the Jews at Mount Sinai through Moses has been superseded by the covenant with Jesus, entered into by faith and baptism in Him.

In recent years a strong movement has developed in the Church that is radically opposed to the continuation of Replacement Theology. Numerous conferences have taken place addressing the dangers of this view. Most who are opposed to Replacement Theology are proponents of the following theological viewpoint.

Remnant Theology
This belief is a total rejection of the concept that God has finished with the Jews or Israel, but it has only developed within the last hundred years or so.

Remnant Theology looks at some of the distinctions that exist between Israel and the Church and rejects the concept that Israel only equals Jews and the Church only equals Gentiles. Key to this whole concept is the teaching of the apostle Paul in Romans chapters 9–11.

Proponents of this belief will not generally refer to it as Remnant Theology, but may instead call themselves Christian Zionists. Central to this theology is the belief that Gentile followers of Jesus are "grafted into" the remnant of Israel, as argued by Paul in Romans 11:17. Here the remnant Israel is portrayed as an olive tree and the Christians are seen as being grafted into it. In verse 18 Paul says something that is totally fundamental to this position: "do not boast over the branches. But if you boast, remember that you do not support the root, but the root supports you" (NET).

In other words, the very root of Christianity is Judaism. The position of most people who hold to this view is that if you destroy the root, you destroy the faith. In other words, without Judaism there is no real Christianity. So the Church is a fundamental part of the remnant of Israel, according to Paul in Romans 11.

While it is essential to understand the theological basis of Remnant Theology, it is just as essential to understand its huge influence in the Church today. The Christian Zionist viewpoint is one of the fastest growing positions in the Church. It may not be so well known in Europe, but in North America it has over 100 million supporters. People often talk about the influence that the Jewish community holds, even though they are a mere 6 million people, forgetting that over 100 million Christians firmly support Israel. Their influence is very significant, particularly politically.

Opponents of those who support Remnant Theology will often accuse them of a lack of care for indigenous Palestinian Christians. Some clearly do need to offer more support for the Palestinians, but many already do – such as the Joseph's Storehouse ministry, led by Messianic Jew Barry Segal. He is an Israeli Jew who accepts Jesus as Messiah, and he has done a huge amount of humanitarian relief work for both Jews and Palestinians. The person who has become the worldwide leader of the Christian Zionist movement is the Texan pastor John Hagee. I think it is important that we have the opportunity to read, in his words, why Christians should support Israel.

Why Christians Should Support Israel

The Apple of His Eye

Everything Christians do should be based upon the biblical text. Here are seven solid Bible reasons why Christians should support Israel.

1. Genesis 12:3: *"And I will bless them that bless thee and curse him that curseth thee; and in thee shall all nations of the earth be blessed."* Point: God has promised to bless the man or nation that blesses the Chosen People. History has proven beyond reasonable doubt that the nations that have blessed the Jewish people have had the blessing of God; the nations that have cursed the Jewish people have experienced the curse of God.

2. Paul recorded in Romans 15:27: *"For if the Gentiles have shared in their* [the Jews'] *spiritual things, they are indebted to minister to them also in material things."* Christians owe a debt of eternal gratitude to the Jewish people for their contributions that gave birth to the Christian faith. Jesus Christ, a prominent Rabbi from Nazareth said, *"Salvation is of the Jews!"*

(John 4:22). Consider what the Jewish people have given to Christianity:

- The Sacred Scripture

- The Prophets

- The Patriarchs

- Mary, Joseph, and Jesus Christ of Nazareth

- The Twelve Disciples

- The Apostles

3. It is not possible to say, "I am a Christian" and not love the Jewish people. The Bible teaches that love is not what you say, but what you do (1 John 3:18). "A bell is not a bell until you ring it, a song is not a song until you sing it, love is not love until you share it."

4. While some Christians try to deny the connection between Jesus of Nazareth and the Jews of the world, Jesus never denied his Jewishness. He was born Jewish, He was circumcised on the eighth day in keeping with Jewish tradition, He had his Bar Mitzvah on his 13th birthday, He kept the law of Moses, He wore the Prayer Shawl Moses commanded all Jewish men to wear, He died on a cross with an inscription over His head, "King of the Jews!" Jesus considered the Jewish people His family. Jesus said (Matthew 25:40), *"Verily I say unto you, inasmuch as you have*

done it unto one of the least of these my brethren
[the Jewish people... Gentiles were never called His
brethren], *ye have done it unto me."*

5. *"Pray for the peace of Jerusalem, they shall prosper
that love thee"* (Psalm 122:6). The scriptural principle
of prosperity is tied to blessing Israel and the city of
Jerusalem.

6. Why did Jesus Christ... [enter] Capernaum and heal
[the centurion's servant], who was ready to die? What
logic did the Jewish elders use with Jesus to convince
Him to come into the house of a Gentile and perform
a miracle? The logic they used is recorded in Luke
7:5: *"For He loveth our nation, and He hath built us a
synagogue."* The message? This Gentile deserves the
blessing of God because he loves our nation and has
done something practical to bless the Jewish people.

7. Why did God the Father select the house of
Cornelius in Caesarea (Acts 10) to be the first Gentile
house in Israel to receive the Gospel? The answer
is given repeatedly in Acts 10. Acts 10:2: *"A devout
man* [Cornelius], *and one that feared God with all
his house, which gave much alms to the people, and
prayed to God always."* Who were the people to
whom Cornelius gave these alms? They were the Jews.
Again in Acts 10:4: *"... thy prayers and thine alms are
come up for a memorial before God."* Again in Acts

10:31: *"... and thine alms are had in remembrance in the sight of God."* The point is made three times in the same chapter. A godly Gentile who expressed his unconditional love for the Jewish people in a practical manner was divinely selected by heaven to be the first Gentile house to receive the Gospel and the first to receive the outpouring of the Holy Spirit. These combined Scriptures verify that PROSPERITY (... Psalm 122:6), HEALING (Luke 7:1–5) and the OUTPOURING OF THE HOLY SPIRIT came first to Gentiles that blessed the Jewish people and the nation of Israel in a practical manner.

We support Israel because all other nations were created by an act of men, but Israel was created by an act of God! The Royal Land Grant was given to Abraham and his seed through Isaac and Jacob with an everlasting and unconditional covenant (Genesis 12:1–3; 13:14–18; 15:1–21; 17:4–8; 22:15–18; 26:1–5 and Psalm 89).

From John Hagee's website: http://www.jhm.org

It cannot be denied that this is a huge and growing movement of great influence within the Church. While this theology has been the response of many evangelicals to the *Shoa*, the response of many mainstream Christians has been the development of Recognition Theology.

Recognition Theology

This theology developed in response to the Holocaust/ *Shoa*, when theologians began asking the question, "How could this have happened in the midst of Christian Europe?" The formation of the International Council of Christians and Jews played an important role in the development of this viewpoint. At its heart was the ten points of the Seelisberg Conference of 1947, mentioned earlier. The history of this event can be found in *The History of the ICCJ*, written by two important members, the late Revd W. W. Simpson and Mrs Ruth Weyl, now in her late eighties. She was very influential in my own journey of discovery about Jewish–Christian relations.

Those who hold to Recognition Theology believe that both Judaism and Christianity are a valid means of salvation. It is a position that has gained some support from both Catholic and Protestant theologians and has even been accepted by some European Protestant churches as their official position.

Recognition Theology supporters set out to examine whether Judaism on its own was a valid means of salvation (they eventually concluded that it was). They recognized the historic role of Judaism in the establishment of the Christian faith – that at the heart of Christianity was not only Jesus the Jew, but thousands of years of salvation history, beginning with Abraham. They asserted that without Judaism, Christianity in the New Testament could not even be properly understood.

Then, in the 1990s, Dr Jacobus Schoneveld, Secretary General of the ICCJ, carried out some important work on the issue of the *Logos* (the Greek for the "Word" found in the prologue of John's Gospel) and the Torah. His conclusion was that the *Logos* and the Torah were one and the same, and therefore salvation could be gained by Jesus the *Logos* or the Torah.

The foundational statement of Judaism is the *Shema*, the nearest thing that Judaism has to a creed. It is an affirmation of what Judaism is, and it comes from Deuteronomy 6:4. Every Jew is obligated to say it, morning and night. The *Shema* is a declaration of faith in one God. It begins, *"Shema Yisrael Adonai eloheinu Adonai ehad"* ("Hear, O Israel: the Lord our God, the Lord is one"). The words are also found on the little scroll in each *mezzuah* attached to the doorpost of every Jewish home. Here the passage is longer, and is taken from verses 4–9 of Deuteronomy 6:

> Hear, O Israel: The Lord our God, the Lord is one.
> Love the Lord your God with all your heart and
> with all your soul and with all your strength. These
> commandments that I give you today are to be on your
> hearts. Impress them on your children. Talk about
> them when you sit at home and when you walk along
> the road, when you lie down and when you get up. Tie
> them as symbols on your hands and bind them on your
> foreheads [the origin of phylacteries]. Write them on
> the doorframes of your houses and on your gates.

The thing common to the *Shema* and the Christian faith is simply the love of God. Jesus Himself, when asked what the greatest commandment was, mentioned the *Shema*.

Conclusion

So the greatest historical division between faiths and races has been that of two people groups with the same heritage: Jews and Christians. As we have briefly reviewed the long, complex history of their interaction, we are reminded that without the root, the branches will surely perish. Much of Christianity has attempted to thrive without its root. Yet, there has always remained a small, faithful group, a remnant in each generation, who have kept alight a holy respect for God's chosen nation.

As I write this, sitting in my room in Baghdad, Iraq, I never dreamt that I would end up working in an Islamic section of the Middle East. My background and my academic interests are steeped in Judaism. Yet even here in Baghdad, Jewish history surrounds me. In Iraq there is one of the longest Jewish histories in the world. Babylon (modern-day Iraq) was the place where the Jews were sent in exile by Nebuchadnezzar. Today, only a handful of Jews remain here, but as little as sixty years ago Iraq had one of the biggest Jewish communities in the world.

I am often asked which of the above theological positions I hold to personally. I can easily say that it is not Replacement Theology, which I passionately believe has been the cause of so much devastation. Even writing about it in this book has once again driven me to tears. At the same time, I give thanks to the Almighty for enabling me to study the Torah and to live out Judaism; to learn to love Judaism with all my heart. I am a follower of a Jew born in Bethlehem who, when asked, "What is the great commandment?", responded, "*Shema Yisrael Adonai eloheinu Adonai ehad*" – "Hear, O Israel: the Lord our God, the Lord is one."

I find it incredibly sad that the radical anti-Judaic polemic has found a new foundation in the past few decades. So many of the Christians have rightly become concerned about their plight in the Middle East and it appears that Israel and its government has increasingly become the focus of its concern. While these people will deny that they are in any way anti-Semitic, their continual bombardment of Israel can be seen as being blatantly anti-Judaic. On the other hand, there will often be a total support for the Palestinian political cause.

This whole movement is increasingly well organized, with support from major Christian ecumenical bodies such as the World Council of Churches. A body called the Ecumenical Accompaniment Program in Palestine and Israel (EAPPI) very much encourages the pilgrimage industry to home in on engagement with Palestinians in the West Bank. The leaders of so many of the churches in the Holy Land have, in essence, become more political than theological leaders. They are often seen as being more political than many of the Islamic leaders. There are many Christians who have been caught up in the ongoing conflict. When it comes to groups like EAPPI, they continually refer to the problems at the checkpoints. I cannot deny that they are real, but when I compare them to what we endure each day in Iraq, they are very insignificant.

What is so important is that the majority of those who hold to this position do not have the support of the majority of Christians on the ground in Palestine. The Christians often feel very removed from their spiritual leaders. Many of the ordinary Palestinian Christians talk warmly and positively about the time when their areas were controlled by Israel. They will speak about the days when they could be treated in Israeli hospitals. Those who live inside the original Israeli borders are considered Israeli Arabs. Many of them have a history that goes back many hundreds of years. The Christians talk about their origin being from Jesus Himself. It is therefore not surprising that churches such as the Syrian Orthodox Church refer to their first bishops as "the Jewish Bishops", acknowledging that most of the early Christians were in fact Jewish.

While one does acknowledge the very real difficulties of the Palestinian Christian community and the Jewish community, we cannot deny that the real tension is between the Western Christian community and the Israeli Jewish community. So many of the Western churches have come out with the most vehemently anti-Israel statements, which look so much like the anti-Judaic polemic of years past. Many ongoing conflicts rear their heads repeatedly in different generations. The really sad fact about this is that it seems as though the evil of anti-Semitism has again reared its ugly head, though it is dressed as a call for justice and liberation for the Palestinians. Let us look at a series of these disputes and statements from different churches.

There have been widespread claims that Israel is involved in ethnic cleansing, and there has been so much opposition against Israel that the Israeli Government has even declared that the churches are rising up against them. This ecclesiastical opposition has come from both Europe and the USA, involving a multitude of denominations in both continents, including the Presbyterians, Lutherans, Anglicans, Methodists, Baptists, the United Church of Christ and the Roman Catholics. As an Anglican, I will begin by looking at the anti-Israel activity of my own denomination.

In recent years there have been a large number of decisions taken by a wide variety of Deanery and Diocesan Synods that have condemned Israel for the way it has treated Palestinians. Motion upon motion has been passed calling for disinvestment and for a cessation of relationships with Israel. Always it is related to how the Palestinians are being treated by the Israelis. There have been countless terrorist and rocket attacks against Israel, but very little is ever said about them.

What causes particular concern is when there is a motion before the General Synod of the Church of England. The Synod only meets two or three times a year, and in its July 2012 meeting it had one such worrying motion. This time it called for the formalization of the Church's relationship with the EAPPI (the Ecumenical Accompaniment Program in Palestine and Israel) – the very body which has been at the forefront of the development of the radical anti-Judaic polemic (which it claims is anti-Israel, not anti-Judaic). The Jewish community do not see it that way.

The motion encouraged church members to participate in the program so they could begin to understand the reality of "life under occupation" and to use the experience of returning participants among the masses. The EAPPI was founded by the World Council of Churches and so has international support. In the UK it has the support of one of the UK's biggest Christian NGOs, Christian Aid. They are accused by the Jewish community of not just being anti-Israel advocates, but of also being responsible for causing widespread anti-Jewish sentiments. The result of this motion was a serious outcry by the Jewish community, including criticism from the chief rabbi, Lord Jonathan Sacks, one of the greatest friends of the Christian community. He made a very important statement:

The work of EAPPI does not provide its participants with a full reflection of the conflict. It presents a one-sided narrative on a complex and difficult issue. It thus fails the test of natural justice: "*Audi alteram partem* – listen to the other side.*" By minimising Israel's well-founded fears, it will not advance the cause of peace or an end to the conflict.

From the Chief Rabbi's website: www.chiefrabbi.org

For true reconciliation to happen, we must always listen to the other side.

Sadly, this negativity from Anglicanism towards Israel has not just occurred in the UK. In the USA the majority of the Episcopal Church have been even more radical but this position has been strongly opposed by the presiding bishop, Katherine Jefferts. On 14 October 2011 fifteen leading Protestant churches in the USA wrote to Congress saying they would be undertaking an immediate investigation into Israeli human rights abuses. The leaders of these churches signed the letter. The noticeable exception was Katherine Jefferts. The anti-Israel Episcopalians implored her to sign the letter, but she declined. As a result of the letter, seven major US Jewish organizations cancelled a significant event of inter-faith activity in which they were all supposed to be participating. Meanwhile, "Episcopalians for Middle East Peace" organized a major online petition to try to get the presiding bishop to sign the anti-Israel declaration.

She still refused. What is more, the subsequent Episcopal General Convention also dismissed overwhelmingly a call for divestment in Israel. As a result, the leaders of the Episcopal Church in the USA stood firmly in support of both the Israelis and the Palestinians, calling for the support of all true peacemakers.

The refusal to listen to the other side is one of the greatest causes of conflict and division and, sadly, it has been a major feature in the continuation of the radical anti-Judaic polemic. This time, however, there is the constant cry that it has nothing to do with Jews outside Israel. Yet, it is very difficult to separate Jews from Israel, since their homeland lies at the very heart of their identity. It is often said that Judaism is about three things: God, Torah and Israel. Historically, we see that this is indeed the case.

As we look at other denominations around the world, we once again see the connection with EAPPI. Always there is the call for boycotts, divestment, and sanctions, causing the movement to become known as BDS. Almost every denomination has pronounced motions calling for radical BDS against Israel. Major churches in the USA, such as the Presbyterians, have been intimately involved in the call for BDS against Israel. The General Assembly of the American Presbyterian Church (GAAPC), at its 217th annual conference, attended by 500 delegates from throughout the USA, stated that there were in-depth discussions going on about major and total disinvestment from Israel and the "occupied territories". Companies that function in these areas are referred to as those that are "consolidating" Israeli occupation and "providing tools for violence and the destruction of Israel". Here the remarks were not just against Palestine but overtly against Israel, which is not even seen as belonging to the Jewish people.

Similarly, the United Church of Christ has

> approved the divestment of companies that help in building the "apartheid wall" or settlements or support the occupation... Thus, while some Arabs move away from the Palestinian cause, we have to appreciate the solidarity moves by the churches, and stand in respect to all those who stand with the utmost courage and defiance side by side with Palestine. They, and we, condemn Israel's crimes and Washington's support for them, and call for their political and military leaders to be brought before international tribunals on war crimes charges.

> **From www.middleeastmonitor.com**

This in itself is a radical anti-Israel statement accusing Israel of nothing less than "war crimes". I firmly believe that many church factions must radically re-evaluate their position on Israel if we are truly going to promote peace and hope for the future.

The sad fact is that 2,000 years after the establishment of Christianity, the walls between Jews and Christians are still horrendous. There may have been some major reconciliation, but there has also been a new division. The establishment of the State of Israel created a justification for a new anti-Judaic polemic (though it is not called anti-Judaism or anti-Semitism, but rather anti-Israel). It has resulted in a huge rift between those who support Israel and those who do not – a rift that, even among Christians, has caused a major theological divide.

For those who support Israel, there is the constant referral to Genesis 12:1–3:

> The Lord had said to Abram, "Go from your country, your people and your father's household to the land I will show you. I will make you into a great nation, and I will bless you; I will make your name great, and you will be a blessing. I will bless those who bless you, and whoever curses you I will curse; and all peoples on earth will be blessed through you."

For those who take a purely Palestinian stance, there is the constant cry that the Israelis are involved in the persecution of the minority in order to increase and justify their own Israeli political position. There are a few Palestinian Christians who have further developed the Palestinian Theology of Liberation mentioned earlier, making their stance clear to many churches by calling for their position to be transparent among many denominations. The division between Jews and Christians today remains huge. The reconciliation work of groups like the ICCJ has been outstanding, but sadly, its members are few compared with those who are against Israel and therefore causing huge tensions between Jews and Christians.

The situation may not be as bad as the time of the *Shoa* in the Second World War, but we are in the middle of a huge crisis and things are getting worse. The new division between Jews and Christians is so subtle and yet so severe. Christians are justifying their anti-Israel position because they are on the side of "the marginalized and the oppressed". Just as in the past they thought they were right about their wrong interpretation of Scripture, so now they are similarly dogmatic regarding their current conceptual understanding.

So we are faced with a true crisis between Jews and Christians. At the heart of reconciliation is the need for all Christians to take seriously their relationship with the Jewish people. After all, our Messiah came as a Jew. Our salvation history is in and through the Jewish people. It begins here in Iraq with the birth of Abraham in Ur, and continues along his lineage until Jesus comes to us as Messiah. Without a basic understanding of Judaism, there can be no understanding of even the fundamentals of the Christian faith. In response to this crisis, I can only think of the response in the Coventry Litany of Reconciliation: "Father, forgive."

CHAPTER 7

Covetousness

*The covetous desires of people and nations
to possess what is not their own,*

Father, forgive.

Having addressed the issue of the hatred between one nation and another that results in division, the Litany of Reconciliation goes on to address six aspects of human sinfulness that further marginalize and minimize our valuing of others, resulting in a rift in relationships and ultimately conflict. The first of these is covetousness – a sin that is referred to in the Ten Commandments. So many of the conflicts in the world are caused by covetousness.

Covetousness has a wide range of expression, depending on its context. In biblical usage it can mean:

1. To gain dishonestly (Exodus 18:21; Ezekiel 33:31).
2. A persistent desire to have more than one currently

    possesses (Luke 12:15; 1 Thessalonians 2:5).

3. An inordinate love of money (Luke 16:14; 2 Timothy
   3:2; Hebrews 13:5).
4. A form of idolatry (Colossians 3:5).
5. The root of many other forms of sin (1 Timothy 6:9–
   10; 2 Kings 5:22–25; Joshua 7:21; Ezekiel 22:12).

In simple terms, covetousness is desiring something that is not ours. It is wanting something so much that we lose our contentment in God, forgetting the truth that "godliness with contentment is great gain" (1 Timothy 6:6).

History has proven that people frequently desire to possess that which is not their own and that, when they act on such desires, it results in strife and conflict.

Covetousness is expressed corporately when one nation exerts its will to possess the land or citizens of another nation. But it operates in individuals before it is expressed corporately. Often people are only concerned with addressing international conflicts at a macro level, but of course, what we are really dealing with is many individuals who want something that does not belong to them.

I write at the moment from Iraq, a nation that saw incredible covetousness under Saddam Hussein. It was nothing more than covetousness that caused him to lead his country to invade Kuwait. He became obsessed with the idea that their land and their oil should be his.

This covetousness led to the Gulf War in 1990–91.

After gaining independence from the United Kingdom in 1932, the Iraqi Government immediately declared that Kuwait was rightfully a territory of Iraq, as it had been associated with Basra until the British creation of Kuwait after the First World War. The Iraqi Government thus stated that Kuwait was a British imperialist invention.

Iraq also accused Kuwait of exceeding its OPEC quotas for oil production. Kuwait persistently overproduced, and the result was a slump in the price of oil. The Iraqi Government described this as a form of economic warfare, since it equated to a yearly $7 billion loss to Iraq.

In early July 1990, Iraq continued to complain about Kuwait's behaviour, in particular its failure to respect its quota. Then Iraq openly threatened to take military action. Then, on 2 August 1990, Iraq launched an invasion by bombing the Kuwaiti capital. Needless to say, as Coalition forces moved to intervene, the ensuing war resulted in thousands of deaths – including those of many innocent civilians.

The sad thing for the ordinary people of Iraq is that Saddam's covetousness led to their nation being subject to thirteen years of radical sanctions imposed by other states, which nearly broke the nation. Iraq continued to decline, and then came the war of 2003. Once again the nation was shattered and, to this day, has not really recovered.

So many wars around the world have been fought because one nation wants, or feels it has a right to, what another nation has. It may be because of the natural resources that the country possesses, or it may be simply because there is a desire to increase territory or to demonstrate that one nation's power is greater than the other's.

It is my observation that covetousness is the one sin that people tend to deny they are even committing. Other sins are more obvious. We can't deny it when we make other things in life a priority over our relationship with God. Others will be able to see this quite plainly in our lives. Covetousness is much more subtle, since our true attitudes often lie hidden. The tenth commandment (Deuteronomy 5:21) reads:

> You shall not covet your neighbour's wife. You shall
> not set your desire on your neighbour's house or
> land, his male or female servant, his ox or donkey, or
> anything that belongs to your neighbour.

The commandment speaks about people, land and possessions. In modern language it might read, "your neighbour's car or tractor". It is referring to things a person might want in order to get around or do their work – things that make for an easier life. The root of covetousness is *dissatisfaction*. It sets seed when we begin to look at what others have and unfavourably compare it with what we have ourselves. It occurs when we convince ourselves that having something will provide us with complete satisfaction, which in turn leads to conflict, whether internal or external. Covetousness always results in us desiring something more than our relationship with God, and therefore effectively replaces Him with the object of our desire. In that respect the first and last commandments that "enclose" the rest are in a similar vein: "You shall have no other gods before me" and "You shall not covet" (Deuteronomy 5:7, 21).

Paul wrote in Colossians 3:5, "Put to death, therefore, whatever belongs to your earthly nature: sexual immorality, impurity, lust, evil desires and greed, which is idolatry." Here covetousness and idolatry are intrinsically linked. It is humanity saying, "I can do this myself; I can get what I need myself. I do not need anything else." It is idolatry because it is placing oneself above God as our ultimate provider.

A much misinterpreted Bible verse, 1 Timothy 6:10, reads, "the love of money is a root of all kinds of evil." This passage does not say that money or wealth is wrong, but focuses on the attitude of our heart. When we covet – when we love something more than God – then it results in evil. Paul continues, "Some people, eager for money, have wandered from the faith and pierced themselves with many griefs." It shows how wrong desires inevitably lead us down a path of suffering, for ourselves and others. The antidote is given in verse 11: "But you, man of God, flee from all this, and pursue righteousness, godliness, faith, love, endurance and gentleness."

This is the challenge of faith: to be continually resting

in the presence of God and walking before Him with a Christlike attitude, so that we are satisfied with His provision in our lives and can live at peace with ourselves and others. The avoidance of covetousness requires a true fight of faith, as we are continually faced with the temptation to:

1. Desire more – because we believe the lie that we never have enough. The more we want, the less satisfied we will be with God's provision for our life.
2. Destroy our spirituality – because covetousness creates a blockage in our relationship with God and stems the flow of His blessing in our life, since He is no longer our satisfaction.
3. Develop further sin – because covetousness is the breeding ground for numerous other sins. It is the foundation for breaking all the other commandments.
4. Destroy our future – because covetousness takes our focus away from who we are destined to be in Christ and diminishes our future potential. "For we brought nothing into the world, and we can take nothing out of it" (1 Timothy 6:7).

Covetousness destroys because it eats away at a person's soul. It affects individuals and individuals affect entire societies, leading to brokenness and conflict. A path to avoid this road has been made available to us, however, because our Lord, in His greatest moment of pain said, "Father, forgive..."

CHAPTER 8

Greed

*The greed which exploits the work of
human hands and lays waste the earth,*

Father, forgive.

Personal greed

At one level, greed and covetousness appear to be very
similar. The distinction that sets them apart is that while
covetousness desires that which belongs to others, greed
desires *more* of that which we already have, as well as
desiring something that does not belong to us. Greed is
an insatiable desire for *more*. The devastation brought
about by greed is similar to the effects of covetousness,
but there are several specific differences.

Among Jesus' teaching, the parable that speaks of
greed more than any other is the familiar story of the
prodigal son in Luke 15. It speaks not only of a wayward

son acting foolishly, but reveals a young man consumed by greed who forgets his father. Showing contempt and disrespect for his father, the young man sees him only as the person who will provide him with his inheritance and, therefore, the means with which to live his life as he sees fit.

The father in the story, out of a generous heart, gives his son his rightful share of the family estate before he is due it. What follows is a sad tale as we observe the downward spiral of the boy from a "man of means", the life and soul of the party, to degrading himself performing the lowest form of manual labour of Jesus' day, especially for a Jew – tending a pig pen. Eventually the boy returns to his father in a dismal state, but his father, representing the Almighty in His grace, welcomes him back with both love and a total reassurance of his continuing status as a son.

The prodigal demonstrates greed in that he eagerly grasps at what he presumes to be his. Although he would receive his inheritance in time, he wants it *now*. As with covetousness, his desire is motivated by the belief that if only he has more, it will result in him being happier and more fulfilled. In reality, his "happiness" was extremely short lived. Those he assumed were his friends deserted him as soon as the money ran out. He ended up living below the poverty line with literally nothing to his name.

Jesus also shows us in the parable the scope of greed and how one person's behaviour causes a ripple effect that impacts the lives of others. The prodigal's greed is a cause of brokenness not just to himself, but to his brother, who resents the grace being shown to him by his father.

The father in the story, too, would have been deeply affected by his son's behaviour. In the first century, an older Middle Eastern man never ran. To do so, he would have to hitch up his tunic and bare his legs – something that culturally was considered shameful and humiliating. Usually, when a Jewish son absconded and lost his inheritance among the Gentiles and then returned home, the community would perform a ceremony called the *kezazah*. They would break a large pot in front of the culprit and declare, "You are now cut off from your people!" The community would then totally reject him.

Why does the father run? It is likely he does so in order to reach his son before he enters the village. The father runs and shames himself so that he can reach his son before the rest of the village, to save *him* from the coming shame and humiliation. How like our Lord, to come looking for us before we go looking for Him.

Dealing radically with personal greed

Just by considering this simple parable, we can see the kind of damage that greed can cause at a micro-relational level. Looking wider, it is easy to see, in a broken world, the extent of the damage and division caused by greed on a macro level.

Greed is utterly self-serving. Its only concern is for self and gaining more. It is all about self-consumption. "What can I get for me?" Greed does not consider the needs of others.

We cannot go anywhere in the world without encountering those in need. As I go about my work in Baghdad, I am constantly engrossed in the needs of others. There is profound poverty here; many people lack basic medical care and need food just to survive. As a church, we accept that we have a duty in meeting the needs of the poor. There is no way the overwhelming needs we are faced with can be met purely by us here in Iraq, but our larger Christian family around the world is astounding as, time and time again, they give in order to help the poor and desperate. That generosity enables us to be a conduit of blessing to those who need it most and allows us to demonstrate the love of Christ in a practical and tangible way.

The need with which I am faced day by day stands in stark contrast to the materialism that exists in the West. So many are driven by the idea that success in life is related to our possessions. How much do we earn each year? How much do we own? Sadly, even the Church has not been exempt from this. There has been a growth in the theological viewpoint known as the "prosperity gospel", which, in very simple terms, promotes the idea that if we do A, B and C, God will be obliged not only to provide for our needs, but also to bless us in increasing measure. The A, B and C usually involve giving to God, but the teaching is always couched in terms of us gaining more as a result: give in order to gain.

God does require us to give out of our resources to Him and He does indeed promise to bless us. But fundamentally, this process is not some kind of legalistic mechanism – if we tick the right boxes God will *have* to bless us. Rather, we are blessed by coming into alignment with His will, where we will be appropriately positioned to receive His blessing.

For me, the choice is simple: the "prosperity gospel" or God's gospel. I have never written much about my own attitude towards giving, but now I think it is right to do so. Giving, in whatever form, is central to my life, church and ministry. I always paid my tithe when I was in a salaried position. Personally, I understood this to be an indisputable biblical command.

Ma'aser, the Hebrew word for "tithe", appears in the Hebrew Scriptures twelve times, but whether it is a clear injunction for us to always give that much is far from clear. The only time Jesus mentioned the tithe was during a rebuke to the religious leaders: "But woe to you Pharisees! For you tithe mint and rue and all manner of herbs, and pass by justice and the love of God. These you ought to have done, without leaving the others undone" (Luke 11:42, NKJV).

When I left paid employment as a canon of Coventry Cathedral, I began working for the new foundation I had established for reconciliation and relief in the Middle East. St George's, Baghdad had already become my church base. I was initially paid by the foundation, but one day God said to me very clearly, "I do not want you to be paid any more." I knew without doubt that it was God speaking, so I knew I had to obey. The only thing I was worried about was telling my wife, Caroline. I did so, and to my total surprise, she told me that for two years she had been praying that I would truly live by faith. She knew what I had to do before I did.

The way I had previously functioned was first to pay my children's school fees and then provide for the basic needs of the family. I have since gone far beyond the concept of tithing. The prayer from the Eucharistic Service simply says, "All that I have is yours and of your own do I give." If everything is already His, then everything belongs to Him. Therefore I do not think that tithing is enough. My policy may not be about providing for me, but it is simply giving to God what is His anyway. I live and work in a community that has nothing. The poverty of our people is quite unbelievable. Every time before I return to Iraq, Lesley, my PA, knows that she has to almost empty my account and give me the money to take to Iraq with me.

At the same time I see how God has met all of my needs. The biggest responsibility I have is to pay for my boys' school fees. When I knew that I would not be paid any more, I confess I was worried about this more than anything. I knew in theory that I did not need to be; I knew that my Father owns the cattle on a thousand hills and that He has promised to provide all my needs according to His riches in glory. But it was still difficult.

The week after making the decision to live purely by faith, I was speaking in Washington, DC. I didn't know anyone in the congregation, but afterwards a lady approached me and said that she wanted to support me and my family personally. After talking to her for a while, it became clear that she wanted to pay *all* of the boys' school fees. Since that day, several years ago, she has paid $75,000 a year to cover their education. This was my biggest lesson in life in trusting my Lord as my Provider.

It is hard to think about acting out of greed in the face of such unmerited grace. I began to realize that, truly, nothing I had was mine; it all belonged to the Almighty, who had promised to provide – and He did! Since then I have given away all I have financially, and God has consistently provided for all my needs. As one West Indian lady used to say to me in the church where I first served, "It does not matter if you give too much to God because He always gives it back."

This is not the "prosperity gospel", which is all about getting what one desires; this is about giving to God freely, knowing that He will provide for all of our needs in His way, in His time. A radical way of dealing with greed from a Christian point of view is simply to see everything we have as His, and give it all to Him! If you give "too much", God will simply give it back.

Greed does not give to God what is rightfully His. This does not apply only to money, but extends to so much else that we posses. People are greedy when it comes to their time. They see their time as a sacred right, a resource which belongs purely to them. Of course, everyone needs time to themselves for rest and relaxation or times of solitude, but it is a form of greed when we are unwilling to share our time selflessly with others.

Last year a senior bishop came to visit us in Iraq. On leaving he said to me, "I cannot see how you manage, having absolutely no spare time. People are with you non stop." This is true. As I write, it is past midnight and I have only just begun my writing for today. My room here acts as my bedroom, my dining room and, indeed, an office for my whole team! In addition, late at night, it is my place of prayer and solitude. Personally, I am grateful for having been given the gift of loving to be with other people. I am a very institutionalized individual. This is not a newly developed attribute; I have always been that way, ever since I was a child. I accept, however, that many people do not find giving lots of time to others as easy as I do – my own dear wife being one of them. Despite us all needing our own time, we cannot hold on to it in a way that engenders greed. Jesus sought solitude at times, but He gave large amounts of His time over to simply being with people.

The ecological impact of greed

Greed has been a major factor in the devastation of large parts of God's creation, such as the damage to the ecosystem caused by the destruction of the rainforests. Left unchecked, greed could lay the earth to waste. When the Coventry Litany was first written, no one could have foreseen the extent of the complex environmental issues that face us today.

Whether we call it the environmental movement, the green movement or the ecological movement, there is a growing desire to protect God's creation – though most would perhaps not think it has anything to do with God. The Bible clearly illustrates how important the welfare of His creation is to God, so it should be important to us too. God is intimately involved with every aspect of His creation. Consider the following Scripture verses.

1. God is the Creator

In the beginning God created the heavens and the earth... God saw all that he had made, and it was very good (Genesis 1:1, 31).

You made the heavens, even the highest heavens, and all their starry host, the earth and all that is on it, the seas and all that is in them. You give life to everything, and the multitudes of heaven worship you (Nehemiah 9:6).

2. *The Earth is the Lord's*

The earth is the Lord's, and everything in it, the world, and all who live in it; for he founded it on the seas and established it on the waters (Psalm 24:1–2; cf. Psalm 89:11; 1 Corinthians 10:26).

To the Lord your God belong the heavens, even the highest heavens, the earth and everything in it (Deuteronomy 10:14).

3. *God loves His creation*

The Lord is good to all; he has compassion on all he has made... The Lord is trustworthy in all he promises and faithful in all he does (Psalm 145:9, 13; cf. Psalm 14).

God saw all that he had made, and it was very good (Genesis 1:31).

4. *He sustains the life of His creation*

In his hand is the life of every creature and the breath of all mankind (Job 12:10).

You care for the land and water it; you enrich it abundantly. The streams of God are filled with water to provide the people with corn, for so you have ordained it. You drench its furrows and level its ridges; you soften it with showers and bless its crops. You crown the year with your bounty, and your carts overflow with abundance. The grasslands of the wilderness overflow; the hills are clothed with gladness. The meadows are covered with flocks and the valleys are mantled with corn; they shout for joy and sing (Psalm 65:9–13).

5. Creation is reconciled to God

... if my people, who are called by my name, will humble themselves and pray and seek my face and turn from their wicked ways, then will I hear from heaven, and I will forgive their sin and will heal their land (2 Chronicles 7:14).

For the creation waits in eager expectation for the children of God to be revealed. For the creation was subjected to frustration, not by its own choice, but by the will of the one who subjected it, in hope that the creation itself will be liberated from its bondage to decay and brought into the freedom and glory of the children of God (Romans 8:19–21).

These next verses show how God commands us to be good stewards of the environment He has given us to live in, and the result of humans defiling the earth:

6. The Lord commands humanity to care for creation

The Lord God took the man and put him in the Garden of Eden to work it and take care of it (Genesis 2:15).

... you must keep my decrees and my laws... And if you defile the land, it will vomit you out as it vomited out the nations that were before you (Leviticus 18:26, 28).

Do not pollute the land where you are... Do not defile the land where you live and where I dwell, for I, the Lord, dwell among the Israelites (Numbers 35:33–34).

7. Humanity has defiled the Earth

I brought you into a fertile land to eat its fruit and rich produce. But you came and defiled my land and made my inheritance detestable (Jeremiah 2:7).

How long will the land lie parched and the grass in every field be withered? Because those who live in it are wicked, the animals and birds have perished (Jeremiah 12:4).

It will be made a wasteland, parched and desolate before me; the whole land will be laid waste because there is no one who cares (Jeremiah 12:11).

There is no faithfulness, no love, no acknowledgment of God in the land. There is only cursing, lying and murder, stealing and adultery; they break all bounds, and bloodshed follows bloodshed. Because of this the land dries up, and all who live in it waste away; the beasts of the field, the birds in the sky and the fish in the sea are swept away (Hosea 4:1–3).

8. *The results of defiling the Earth*

He turned rivers into a desert, flowing springs into thirsty ground, and fruitful land into a salt waste, because of the wickedness of those who lived there (Psalm 107:33–34).

Woe to you who add house to house and join field to field till no space is left and you live alone in the land. The Lord Almighty has declared in my hearing: "Surely the great houses will become desolate, the fine mansions left without occupants. A ten-acre vineyard will produce only a bath of wine; a homer of seed will yield only an ephah of grain" (Isaiah 5:8–10).

The earth dries up and withers, the world languishes and withers, the heavens languish with the earth. The earth is defiled by its people; they have disobeyed the laws, violated the statutes and broken the everlasting covenant. Therefore a curse consumes the earth; its people must bear their guilt (Isaiah 24:4–6).

The nations were angry, and your wrath has come. The time has come for judging the dead, and for rewarding your servants the prophets and your people who revere your name, both great and small – and for destroying those who destroy the earth (Revelation 11:18).

Despite the clear consequences of defiling God's creation, still His desire is for reconciliation:

9. Reconciliation between God and creation

... ask the animals, and they will teach you, or the birds in the sky, and they will tell you; or speak to the earth, and it will teach you, or let the fish in the sea inform you. Which of these does not know that the hand of the Lord has done this? In his hand is the life of every creature and the breath of all mankind (Job 12:7–10).

The heavens declare the glory of God; the skies proclaim the work of his hands. Day after day they pour forth speech; night after night they reveal knowledge. They have no speech, they use no words; no sound is heard from them. Yet their voice goes out into all the earth, their words to the ends of the world (Psalm 19:1–4; cf. Psalm 97:6).

10. Creation praises the Lord, the Creator

Let the heavens rejoice, let the earth be glad; let the sea resound, and all that is in it. Let the fields be jubilant, and everything in them; let all the trees of the forest sing for joy. Let all creation rejoice before the Lord (Psalm 96:11–13).

Praise the Lord from the heavens; praise him in the heights above. Praise him, all his angels; praise him, all his heavenly hosts. Praise him, sun and moon; praise him, all you shining stars. Praise him, you highest heavens and you waters above the skies. Let

them praise the name of the Lord, for at his command
they were created, and he established them for ever
and ever – he issued a decree that will never pass away
(Psalm 148:1–6).

God's creation is a gift to us and we must care for it
responsibly. The Coventry Litany counsels us that to
live the life of a reconciler, we must avoid the greed that
leads to the devastation of our natural resources.

Economic greed and poverty

So much of the conflict in the world is driven by an
underlying economic greed. Nations, if they cannot
generate sufficient wealth for themselves, are liable to
exploit other, more vulnerable nations. Within nations,
social, ethnic and class divides, along with black-market
economies, mean that certain groups of people in society
are cruelly exploited for the financial gain of other groups
of people. People trafficking for the sex and drug trades
are two obvious examples of exploitation for financial
gain due to greed. Greed is prepared to do anything to
get what it wants and the end always justifies the means.
As Mahatma Gandhi once said, "There is sufficiency in
the world for man's need, but not for man's greed."

The past few years have seen many financial
institutions shaken and some of the underlying greed
exposed. Early in 2012, an executive of the investment
bank Goldman Sachs wrote an article in which he

expressed his perception of the bank and of how attitudes have changed over the past decade. In it he wrote, "When I joined the bank 12 years ago it was all about teamwork, integrity, a spirit of humility and always doing right by our clients..." In recent years, he claimed, the bank had been transformed into a place where "callously people talk about ripping their clients off". He concluded by saying that the bank had been "lost underneath a tsunami of greed" (*Daily Telegraph*, 14 March 2012).

There still exists everywhere in the world an unfathomable gulf between the rich and the poor. Almost half the world's population – over 3 billion people – live on less than $2.50 per day. According to UNICEF, 22,000 children die each day due to poverty. And they "die quietly in some of the poorest villages on earth, far removed from the scrutiny and the conscience of the world. Being meek and weak in life makes these dying multitudes even more invisible in death" (www. globalissues.org).

Here in Iraq I am faced with unbelievable poverty day after day, and I witness the consequences that the conflict of nation against nation has brought to the lives of ordinary people. Nine years after Saddam was deposed, the nation is close to being a failed state. The Iraqi state cannot provide basic services for its citizens, including a consistent supply of electricity, clean water and adequate healthcare. The continuing wave of violence, bombings and shootings means that the majority live with constant fear and uncertainty. Most have lost hope for the future.

Nations are rent apart by greed, whether it be environmental, institutional, or as a result of corruption in the acquisition of wealth. If this or any land is to be restored and healed, we must cultivate a new approach – a transformed attitude of good stewardship born out of a respect for others and their possessions, and a wise handling of our own resources. As Socrates once said, "He who is not contented with what he has, would not be contented with what he would like to have."

CHAPTER 9

Envy and Indifference

Our envy of the welfare and happiness of others,

Father, forgive.

Envy

Envy is similar in nature to both covetousness and greed, yet it has its own distinct character and, equally, is a cause of conflict. At the heart of envy is the feeling of discontent that others are in a better position than ourselves. We may envy the prosperity of another and wish it for ourselves, or we may be envious of the fact that they have certain possessions that we do not.

Envy has been at the heart of many conflicts. A good example of this is the problems that have existed between the Iraqis and the Kurds. In theory they are fellow countrymen, living in the same nation, but in practice they are not. Kurdistan, in the north of Iraq, has its own language, flag and government. This area and these people were brutally persecuted under the regime of Saddam Hussein. Five thousand people were massacred in a matter of minutes in one town alone, Halabja, when they were attacked with chemical weapons in 1988. There is a saying among the Kurds that they have "no friends but the mountains" – a reference to that fact that the world has barely taken notice as one aggressor after another has driven these once nomadic tribes deep into the mountains to seek refuge. Resistance against oppression has been a way of life for them.

Kurdistan separated from Iraq after the 1991 invasion of Kuwait. The international community worked to ensure that Kurdistan was treated separately from Iraq, and a no-fly zone was established over the whole of that area. During the twelve years before the 2003 war against Iraq, Kurdistan was transformed into a normal developed country with a good infrastructure. The harvest fields of Kurdistan become more productive each year and she now has a reputation as a producer of vegetables, cereals and fruits of the highest quality. The Kurds are blessed with an agreeable climate, an abundant water supply and rich, fertile soil. If you were to look at the area on a satellite map, you would see that Kurdistan is predominantly green while the rest of Iraq is brown.

The people of Iraq cannot cope with the success and prosperity of Kurdistan. Iraqis live in total and utter chaos and disaster, with extreme poverty and few or no possessions. The general attitude of the average Iraqi to the Kurds is one of envy and negativity. In the words of the Coventry Litany, they are envious of the Kurds' "welfare and happiness".

Envy is something we are all guilty of at one time or another, yet without exception we find it hard to admit it. In trying to understand envy, the great philosopher Socrates is once again helpful:

> Envy is the daughter of pride, the author of murder
> and revenge, the begetter of secret sedition, the
> perpetual tormenter of virtue. Envy is the filthy slime
> of the soul; a venom, a poison, a quicksilver, which
> consumes the flesh and dries up the bones.

Like so many other sins, envy can lead to worse iniquities – such as murder.

Envy is like a poison to the soul because it has to do with a lack of self-acceptance. We envy because we do not accept that we already have all we need. Instead of turning to God as the source of all our needs and our peace and well-being, we begin to look at others and become jealous of their apparent success and prosperity. Scripture commands us to love others as we love ourselves, but the fact is that many people do not love and appreciate themselves. Envy is not seeing ourselves as God sees us. It is the absence of love.

Envy is therefore a matter for reconciliation, because it creates a relational rift between parties. Envy is based upon a fundamental misunderstanding of the other party's position. In reality, we may have little idea why someone else is prospering while we are not – yet we conjecture on the matter, draw our own conclusions, envy them and treat them differently to others, thus creating division.

Envy eats away at the soul. Proverbs 14:30 says, "A heart at peace gives life to the body, but envy rots the bones." As I look around me in Iraq, I see that ultimately terrorism is connected to envy, because terrorism has to do with loss – in this instance, a loss of power. It does not matter, however, whether the loss is to do with power, wealth, possessions or influence. Envy looks at the loss and says, "I want that back", and it is usually at any price.

As we look at the most extreme terrorism in Iraq, we see that it occurs mostly among the Sunnis. They once held ultimate power and authority, and all the benefits that went with that. Their power has been moved to the Shia since the overthrow of the evil Saddam Hussein. The Sunni look at the Shia with great envy, and a few of them are led to be people of conflict and terrorism. It may just be a tiny minority, but the evil and damage that they do is so great that the rest of the world now wrongly thinks all Muslims are terrorists.

In Scripture, envy is identified as one of the factors that are a blockage to salvation and the antithesis of Christian values. In his famous summary in 1 Corinthians 13, Paul lists all the attributes of love. The very first negative character trait he mentions is envy: "Love is patient, love is kind. It does not envy, it does not boast, it is not proud" (verse 4). Similarly, Peter tells us, "rid yourselves of all malice and all deceit, hypocrisy, envy, and slander of every kind" (1 Peter 2:1).

Envy is not just a symptom of a reprobate character. Christians are susceptible to it as much as anyone. Envy is a factor in the conflicts and divisions that exist within churches. People are envious when others (who they may feel are less qualified than themselves) are awarded positions of leadership or responsibility. Instead of harbouring envy, if we feel hurt or offended, our response should simply be, "Father, forgive." Each of us is in need of the grace of God in our lives, and therefore we are called to extend that grace to others. As we humble ourselves before God, He allows us to see that envy will only serve to prevent us from being the people that He has purposed us to be, and from receiving all the blessings that He desires to pour out.

To overcome envy is to be aware of the danger of jealousy and our desire for notoriety and approval. We must deal with our own insecurities and emotional inadequacy by really understanding the depth of the love that God has for us. Escaping the trap of envy is fundamental to our calling to be peacemakers and to our own personal spiritual development.

Indifference

Our indifference to the plight of the imprisoned, the
homeless, the refugee,

Father, forgive.

At this point, the Litany addresses another heart issue
– our indifference. It focuses on how we deal with
those who are despised and rejected; those who are
imprisoned, homeless or refugees.

As I break the bread at communion at St George's, I
say these words:

We break this bread for those who have no bread – the
imprisoned, the homeless, the refugee. We break this
bread to remember the broken child in each of us, and
that one day we and all creation shall be healed. We
break this bread to share in the body of Christ.

These are key words for the most central act of our
Christian faith, and as we celebrate Christ's sacrificial
act on our behalf, we also remember His brokenness. It
is impossible to acknowledge His brokenness without
acknowledging the brokenness of so many around us.
We are called to acknowledge those on the margins of
society – the homeless, the rejected, those forced to flee
their homeland, those in prison. Our natural response to
these people can be so different to Christ's expectation
of us.

People will complain about the cost of incarcerating so many criminals. They complain about homeless tramps degrading the neighbourhood and intruding into their comfortable world. They complain about the refugees who, as they see it, are flooding into their country seeking the good life or to sponge off the welfare system. We get angry because these destitute people are disrupting our nice lives.

Inevitably, I look towards my own people, here in Baghdad. So many do not have and cannot afford food. We give them food each week just to help them survive. Many have suffered persecution, threats and torture, and have therefore been forced to flee to neighbouring countries where they live as asylum seekers in total desperation. Suddenly this Litany of Reconciliation becomes so real. When our Lord Jesus talks about those who will enter the Kingdom of Heaven in Matthew 25:31–40, it is how we have dealt with those on the margins of society that He is speaking about. What we do for others, we do for Him. We are the very hands and feet of Jesus. We are meant to be the very manifestation of the Kingdom of God on earth.

> When the Son of Man comes in his glory, and all the angels with him, he will sit on his glorious throne. All the nations will be gathered before him, and he will separate the people one from another as a shepherd separates the sheep from the goats. He will put the sheep on his right and the goats on his left.

Then the King will say to those on his right,
"Come, you who are blessed by my Father; take your
inheritance, the kingdom prepared for you since the
creation of the world. For I was hungry and you gave
me something to eat, I was thirsty and you gave me
something to drink, I was a stranger and you invited
me in, I needed clothes and you clothed me, I was ill
and you looked after me, I was in prison and you came
to visit me."

Then the righteous will answer him, "Lord, when
did we see you hungry and feed you, or thirsty and
give you something to drink? When did we see you
a stranger and invite you in, or needing clothes and
clothe you? When did we see you ill or in prison and go
to visit you?"

The King will reply, "Truly I tell you, whatever you
did for one of the least of these brothers and sisters of
mine, you did for me."

The truth is, at the heart of our service to others is our
service of the Lord Himself. An authentic Christian faith
is one that demonstrates truth in a tangible way. This
may be by visiting people in prison, becoming involved
in ministry to the homeless on the streets of your town,
or supporting relief agencies who are caring for the
needs of refugees.

However it is expressed, faith must reveal itself
through our humanity in practical acts. When I was

a vicar in London, each week people from our church would go out onto the streets to feed and care for the homeless. My own commitment in this area was to one particular African man. He suffered from mental health problems and had literally nothing to his name. Over several months we became friends and eventually I felt I should invite him to live with me. This was not always easy. I remember one day when I had asked him to go out and buy some food, and he returned with only boxes of birdseed! On another occasion I came home to find that he had taken the front door off its original hinges and turned it around the other way. This went on for months. We eventually helped him to get his own flat, but I remained a part of his life. Often people would find it bizarre that I was committed to this man, but for me it was simply part of the work of God's Kingdom. Taking risks on those people who have been rejected and discarded by others is always a part of serving our Lord Jesus and part of our ministry of reconciliation.

CHAPTER 10

Lust and Pride

The lust which dishonours the bodies of men, women and children,

Father, forgive.

Lust

This is one of the most challenging statements of the Litany we have to consider, and perhaps the hardest of the "seven deadly sins" to deal with. Yet, it is something that affects each one of us personally. We can try to be very clever and abstract when describing the nature of lust, but the fact is, we are mostly talking about unchecked sexual desire. That is the most common expression of lust. Focused in the right direction as an expression of marriage, sexual desire is a gift from God, something beautiful and a powerful relational bond. Channelled in the wrong direction and used in the wrong context, it becomes debased and degraded. The adulteration of a beautiful gift of God can destroy the bodies of men, women and children. Psychologists will try to camouflage uninhibited sexual desire as a complex personal and social phenomenon, but in reality it is nothing more than lust.

One of the biggest challenges to the modern Church is how it deals with lust and communicates the message of its dangers to a society which, in the main, believes that promiscuity is both acceptable and inevitable. Traditional beliefs and values regarding purity and the sanctity of marriage are seen as negative and old-fashioned. For those of us following the Judeo-Christian path of faith, the rules are very clear: all forms of promiscuity are completely unacceptable. Not only do we expect this of ourselves, we expect it of society as a whole.

The Scriptures are very clear: a sexual relationship is reserved purely for those who are married. It is black and white, with no room for manoeuvre. Temptation is not a sin in itself, but giving in to temptation is.

Much has been written and spoken about how one can cope with sexual temptation and lust. I have to admit that my approach is very different to that of most people. My viewpoint may not be very sympathetic, but for me it's very clear. Our Lord calls us not to fall into lust or temptation, and our response must be the same as His when He was tempted: "Get behind me, Satan."

I was recently disturbed by a report that said that 90 per cent of church ministers had viewed pornography on their computer or TV at some point. I find it difficult to believe that things are as bad as this. If it is true, then we are saying that 90 per cent of priests, pastors and ministers cannot be trusted. How can people who engage with such evil really provide any kind of spiritual leadership? Even more terrible are the increasing numbers of priests and ministers who have been found guilty of committing sexual abuse against children. This is one of the worst crimes it is possible for a spiritual leader to commit, since they occupy a position of such responsibility. It is so difficult to forgive such a breach of trust.

Sexual abuse is no longer something that is only directed towards women and children; now men are also targeted. When I was training for ministry I did something that is not allowed to happen now – I went to live in a prison for a month, as a prisoner. The prisoners themselves were not informed that I was not one of them; they just assumed I was a new inmate. I was on a steep learning curve and it was here that I first heard about the horror of the sexual abuse that occurs in male prisons, with men being attacked and raped by other prisoners.

Those who had been sent to prison for sexually abusing children were dealt with very differently to those who had abused adults. In the UK child-abusers are referred to as "nonces" and are often kept in solitary confinement because of the risk to their safety from other prisoners. Often these prisoners came from a different social background to the majority of prisoners, and frequently came from the higher classes. They looked and dressed differently. I looked different too and arrived at prison straight from my Cambridge college, wearing a jacket and tie.

My problems began when I turned up to receive my prison clothes from the prisoners who ran that unit. The first thing said to me was, "Whitey, what you in for?" I wasn't supposed to let on that I wasn't a real prisoner, so I answered vaguely, "Oh, this and that." But later that day these same prisoners approached me. The leader told me in no uncertain terms, "Whitey, we think we know why you're in here. You're a nonce, aren't you? If you don't tell us what you've done we'll smash your face into the ground." I could see that they were really serious, so I had to tell them the truth, that I was training to be a priest and I had been sent to discover what it was really like in prison. "So, you're a man of God!" one of the black prisoners cried. They found it hard to believe that anyone would voluntarily go to prison, but eventually they decided that they couldn't hit me if I really was a man of God.

It was clear to me that in prison, just as in the outside world, there were rules and standards that should not be broken. Prisoners took it upon themselves to punish other prisoners for their "crimes" – the worst of which was being found to have committed abuse against children.

Lust may not be the cause of international conflicts in the same way as covetousness or greed, but it is a source of interpersonal conflict and has ruined many relationships. We appeal to God for His grace and mercy so that we may not fall foul of its trap.

Pride

> The pride which leads us to trust in ourselves and not in God,
>
> **Father, forgive.**

If it were possible to "sum up" the problem of the human condition as expressed in the Litany and describe it in one word, that word would be *pride*. If we could deal ruthlessly with the issue of pride, it would vastly reduce the occurrence of conflict. It would alleviate the tensions that exist between race and class, the hatred that exists between nation and nation. In the end, so much conflict has at its core this attitude: "Who do you think you are? I am better than you!"

If pride were banished, then covetousness would be a thing of the past, since humility nullifies the desire to grasp after that which is not your own. Is not also greed a symptom of pride? Greed says that because of who I am, I deserve more! Envy too is rooted in pride. If we honestly believe we are better than others, then why should they be so happy and have so much, and not us? Pride also leads to the neglect of the marginalized.

It looks at those on the fringes of society and declares, "If they had any sense, they would not have let that happen to them." In other words, if only they could be more like "me", they wouldn't find themselves in such a bad position. It must be their own fault, so why should I care about them? Finally, lust stems from pride too. Pride says to itself, "I am worth more than you, therefore I have a right to get what I want", regardless of how this might use and degrade others.

Scripture warns us that "The fool says in his heart, 'There is no God'" (Psalm 14:1). This verse illuminates an attitude where there is a total reliance on self and no trust in God. Who is the foolish person? The person who is proud enough to presume that life revolves around them. Without thought for the consequences, they blunder through life, committing all of the above sins.

Self-reliance and self-centredness come so naturally to us human beings that no one is exempt from their dangers. Church leaders are just as guilty as anyone, behaving, at times, as though they have God in their pocket and possess the answers to all things – even presuming upon the miraculous and supernatural. One of the most wonderful things about serving among the suffering, persecuted Church is that it teaches you, over and over again, that we have nothing to be proud about. God regularly answers the prayers of little children as much as, if not more than, mine. This keeps me humble.

Knowing that I am absolutely powerless to change people's situations apart from the miraculous intervention of God is both extremely humbling and, at the same time, wonderfully liberating. As I go about my work in the parish, time and again I see God working through the destitute. In our church we regularly see miracles, even the dead being raised. Such miracles happen through the prayers of *all* our people. Each time we have seen someone raised from the dead, it was never me who was doing the praying. Notably, those who were healed had never trusted in the resurrection power of Jesus beforehand. They were all Muslim children. Truly, God uses the meek, destitute and broken to do His work.

Pride continually gets in our way. It prevents us from seeing how great God is and how insignificant we are. People who have nothing and hold no opinion of themselves don't generally suffer with this problem. Therefore the supernatural working of God through them is not hindered. What a lesson for us all!

Pride also prevents us from admitting the full degree of our own sin and wretchedness. We need to come to the end of ourselves, to exhaust our self-sufficiency, so that we may acknowledge our own insignificance. It is only then that we can truly acknowledge God's all-sufficiency and power. Pride keeps us out of the presence of God and thus limits our ability to encounter Him. It stops us from having a deeper relationship with Jesus and being transformed in His presence. It causes us to have an ungodly self-righteousness. So, in our pride we need to ask for true humility and pray, "Father, forgive."

In essence, the Litany is calling for humility – that virtue which, if we think we have it, we don't have it. Humility is the factor that binds us to Christ and enables us to be effective as His hands and feet in the world. Humility enables us to avoid conflict because it desires to put others before oneself. Humility is opposed to pride.

Tender-hearted

Then we come to the very final words of the Litany, which are taken from Paul's letter to the Ephesians (4:32). Here Paul lays out for us how Christians should live:

> Be kind to one another, tender-hearted, forgiving one another, as God in Christ forgave you.

This verse was chosen to conclude the Litany because it summarizes everything to do with the life that followers of Jesus are called to live. We are to emulate the tender-heartedness and forgiveness of Christ.

There are certain times in one's life when you hear words spoken that, immediately, you know you will never forget. One such time occurred for me in 1990. I was at a Christian conference centre belonging to Holy Trinity Brompton. Standing in the grand courtyard, the manager of the centre, Johnny Lavers, was talking to his daughter Jessica before she went to school. I will never forget what he said to her. It was simply, "Remember kindness." He told me that he said this to his daughters every day.

So often since then I have sat down with people engaged in the harshest of conflicts and thought to myself, "If only they would remember kindness." To show *kindness* to another, regardless of whether they deserve it or not, is the epitome of tender-heartedness. It is loving others out of a place of humility, with no hint of pride. The last thing I say to my congregation each week in Baghdad as we close the service is, "*Al Hub, Al Hub, Al Hub*" – "Love, Love, Love." If we can truly love, then we will live by the values of the Litany and we will be ministers of reconciliation.

Conclusion

Father, forgive

Repeated throughout Coventry's Litany of Reconciliation are these two words: "Father, forgive." We remind ourselves that it does not say, "Father, forgive *them*", but simply, "Father, forgive." Central to the Litany is the understanding that it is not just others who need *our* forgiveness. We too are in constant need of forgiveness, as our attitudes fall short of God's glory.

It is a tradition that the words of the Litany are read at the cathedral daily, and on Fridays they are recited in the ruins of the old cathedral. On Friday the Litany is also read at the hundreds of other centres of reconciliation around the world. We say it too, here in Baghdad. Our cross of nails is a symbol of forgiveness and reconciliation in a war-torn land. There can be no reconciliation without forgiveness, as painful as this may be. I repeat here that forgiveness prevents the pain of the past from determining our future.

We have examined the issues highlighted by the Litany as the causes of conflict: hatred, covetousness, greed, envy, indifference to suffering, lust and pride. How do we prevent the dire consequences of these sins? By radically allowing the forgiveness of Jesus to pave the way for rifts to be closed, to bring healing, to work towards reconciliation. Broken communities can be restored by the unconditional love of Christ. In the greatest act of reconciliation, our Lord Jesus cried from the cross, "Father, forgive them; they know not what they do." He was calling for forgiveness for those who had crucified Him.

Lewis Smedes, a former Fuller Theological Seminary lecturer and a prolific author, wrote the book *Forgive and Forget* (HarperSanFrancisco, 2007). In it he states, "When you release the wrongdoer from the wrong, you cut a malignant tumour out of your inner life. You set a prisoner free, but you discover that the real prisoner was yourself." This reminds me that "Father, forgive" is a confession that releases grace to the wrongdoer, but freedom to ourselves. Forgiveness is a process that takes time, but so many cripple themselves by clinging on to the pain of the past, unwilling to relinquish it. Of course, it is not easy to let go of pain, but it surely prevents us from moving forward.

Conflict always results in pain. It may be that our land or property has been attacked or taken from us. We may have been so mentally abused that we can forgive, but we can't escape the pain. But so often, our cry for "justice" is really a cry for what we believe we want or need – which is often a vindictive strike back at the person or people who caused our pain. So often we are consumed with merely "getting back" at those who have hurt us in order to cause them similar suffering. We think about the tragedies here in the Middle East, the loss of land and property suffered by many in Israel and Palestine, or those who endured the terrible chemical bombing in places like Halabja in Kurdistan. There can be a rightful seeking of justice and restoration, but forgiveness is still needed so that we do not continue to live in a place of private bitterness.

The message of Jesus is so radical because it demands that our forgiveness also involves forgetting. When God forgives us, He no longer brings to mind our offences – as if they had never occurred. Similarly, we have to choose to "forgive and forget" – to extend grace and forgiveness and then move on, choosing not to revisit those transgressions.

Luke 6:37 instructs us: "Do not judge, and you will not be judged. Do not condemn, and you will not be condemned. Forgive, and you will be forgiven."

In Matthew 18:21 we see Peter asking Jesus, "Lord, how many times shall I forgive my brother or sister who sins against me? Up to seven times?" Jesus answers, "I tell you, not seven times, but seventy-seven times." Some versions translate this as "seventy times seven". In other words, there should be no limit. Forgiveness is not a one-time-only, easy formula. It is a lifestyle we must cultivate and continuously live out.

In Luke 17:3–5 Jesus states again the extent of forgiveness: "So watch yourselves. If your brother or sister sins against you, rebuke them; and if they repent, forgive them. Even if they sin against you seven times in a day and seven times come back to you saying 'I repent,' you must forgive them." Then the apostles said to Jesus, "Increase our faith!"

Thus, at the very heart of the Christian faith is the message of Jesus to Forgive, Forgive and Forgive.

The work of reconciliation often involves being confronted with the need to forgive those who, naturally, we would prefer not to forgive – murderers, those guilty of monstrous crimes. Yet we are called not only to forgive them personally, but also to help those who have been hurt by them to forgive them too. This is why love and kindness must be working in the heart of the process. Reconciliation is never the easy option and never takes the line of least resistance. But we are all called to be ministers of reconciliation before Christ.

A Reflection

The Principles of Reconciliation

In summary

Reconciliation is at the heart of Christian ministry and we are all called to the ministry of reconciliation.

Reconciliation is about mending that which is broken – restoring relationships to all that they were intended to be.

Jesus taught us to love our enemies – a radical, countercultural statement. Love is reconciliation in practice, because there can be no reconciliation without forgiveness.

At the heart of conflict is the mis-truth that it is always somebody else who is the problem.

The principles of reconciliation

The goal of reconciliation is to heal the rifts caused by conflict.

We must acknowledge that we are ill equipped and inadequate for the task of reconciliation without the help of God.

We begin by restoring communication; then we restore relationship over time.

Reconciliation must have a starting point, so we begin by finding some common ground. We have to embrace the challenge of making friends with our enemies. Who is my enemy? It is the person whose story I have not heard.

We need to listen more than we speak; we need to *really* listen and understand.

Reconciliation requires a practical demonstration of God's love. We need to understand another's needs before we can meet them. Unconditionally meeting the needs of others demonstrates that we are serious about reconciliation.

Simply "being present" and listening will, over time, build trust. Progress cannot be made without a degree of trust, but will be made where some trust exists, however small.

Unity does not mean uniformity or compliance. A degree of compromise is always necessary to move forward into reconciliation.

Above all, *forgive, forgive, forgive* and *love, love, love.*

Pray for Our Ministry

People regularly ask me about the social situation in Iraq today. Here is some information to help you pray for us – which is so appreciated.

As I write this, it has been nine years since the war to liberate Iraq from its evil dictatorship took place. We had hoped that by now Iraq would be on an upward spiral regarding democracy, human rights and religious freedom. Sadly, this is not the case. There is increasing sectarianism, diminishing human rights, no religious freedom and a political system that is mayhem, to say the least.

The sad reality is that the world has forgotten Iraq. The lack of international attention has resulted in its continued, rapid demise. While even under Saddam there was a police force with total control and some order, now that has all gone. Corruption is rife and is present at every level of society, from the most senior government minister to the policeman on the street. In reality, you get what you can pay for. No money equals no power or influence. It is particularly worrying to see how this affects law and order. There is no real law or order.

This has also caused a total lack of human rights, particularly in the legal system, which has resulted in the serious persecution of most people under arrest. If you pay for protection, you get it; if you cannot afford it, you don't get it.

Added to the political and human rights issues, the religious sectarianism issues have not diminished either. The major issue continues to be between Sunni and Shia. The recent warrant for the arrest of Vice President Tariq Al Hashami has only heightened the tension further, with increased attacks on the Shia by the Sunni.

While the recent Sunni fatwa I helped to broker has stopped a lot of the violence, no religious injunction like a fatwa can have any effect against the biggest Sunni terrorist group, AQI (Al Qaida in Iraq).

Originally Baghdad-based, this group has become increasingly Kurdish-based. Nearby Mosul (formerly Nineveh, the original home base of the Christians) has become an increasing centre for terrorist activity. There is no security there or religious freedom. There is no chance of questioning any aspect of religion, as Sunni terrorism is the only position that is permitted. In Mosul there is absolutely no respect for (or adherence to) the UN Declaration on Human Rights. The situation there regarding religious freedom is even worse.

When people ask me how they should pray for us here in Iraq, I ask them to pray for the Three Ps: Protection, Provision and Perseverance. These are all contained within Psalm 23.

Provision

We have to provide many people with food, healthcare, education and much more. We never know where our support will come from each month, but our Lord always provides what we need. Please pray that we may be able to continue to meet these many needs.

The most important thing that we provide is the love of the Almighty. Our most important evangelistic tool continues to be our medical and dental clinic. People receive free treatment and then come to church. We now have so many Muslims in the church that our overflow room can no longer hold all of them. We pray that the Lord will provide a way for us to be able to afford air-conditioning for the room. It is now 45 degrees centigrade, but it will reach 60 degrees by mid summer.

Protection

Though there is very little media coverage about what is happening here, we continue to be under regular attack. People are killed every day and bombs continually explode. Regularly our people are wounded and killed not because they are targeted but because they are in the wrong place at the wrong time. Our church is surrounded by bomb barricades and military security barriers. To enter it is to enter the heart of a war zone.

We thank God that despite all these difficulties, He has provided security for our complex and that so many of our soldiers have come to know Jesus.

Perseverance

It is a miracle that the Lord has enabled us not just to continue in this ministry but to love it. Please pray that no longer will the remaining Christians want to flee the country, but that the Lord will enable them to stay and persevere.

Also by Canon Andrew White:

The Vicar of Baghdad

FIGHTING FOR PEACE IN THE MIDDLE EAST

ISBN: 978 1 85424 876 3 £8.99 UK / $14.99 US

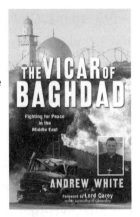

Andrew White is one of a tiny handful of people trusted by virtually every side in the complex Middle East. Political and military solutions constantly fail. Andrew offers a different approach, speaking as a man of faith to men of faith. Compassionate and shrewd, gifted in human relationships, he has been deeply involved in the rebuilding of Iraq.

His first-hand connections and profound insights make this a fascinating document.

"Andrew is, truly, one of the most remarkable men I have ever encountered.... I wholeheartedly commend this book to your attention. It is an inspirational read."
– Lord Carey of Clifton

"Canon Andrew White has fostered the most promising politico-spiritual reconciliation process.... Diplomats who deny the role of religion in political discourse should stay away from the Middle East. Here religion and politics are inextricably linked. Andrew White's work provides vivid evidence that engaging religious leaders is central to any hope of ultimate success in waging peace in the Middle East."
– Bud McFarlane, former National Security Advisor to President Ronald Reagan

"I have known Andrew White for many years and have great admiration for him as a peacemaker. In the face of personal ill-health and threats to his life, he continues his extraordinary work with determination and unrelenting enthusiasm. Not everyone is called to such a ministry but Andrew acts as if he was born to it."
– Revd Nicky Gumbel, HTB

"Andrew White's commitment to working across faiths to secure peace in the Middle East has resulted in this extraordinary book. It charts not just his bravery but that of the people of the Middle East who want a fairer, more secure and more just world. It's a lesson to us all."
– Baroness Amos

Faith Under Fire

WHAT THE MIDDLE EAST CONFLICT HAS TAUGHT ME ABOUT GOD

ISBN: 978 1 85424 962 3 £8.99 UK / $13.99 US

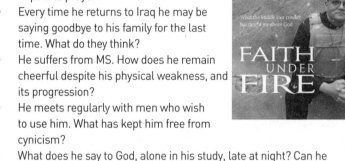

Andrew White, the dedicated "Vicar of Baghdad", encounters daily tragedy.

- What happened to his faith when a young girl in his congregation died, after much hope and prayer?
- Every time he returns to Iraq he may be saying goodbye to his family for the last time. What do they think?
- He suffers from MS. How does he remain cheerful despite his physical weakness, and its progression?
- He meets regularly with men who wish to use him. What has kept him free from cynicism?
- What does he say to God, alone in his study, late at night? Can he see the hand of God? Looking ahead, can he be optimistic about the future? Where are his sources of spiritual energy?

"If anyone has truly had their faith pounded in the fiery crucible of conflict, it is Canon Andrew White. His leadership of the Christian community in Baghdad is quite remarkable. For many, his experiences would have produced anger and bitterness, but for him and his congregation their reaction is the opposite: 'Despite our suffering,' he writes, 'we are not miserable, but joyful!' This book explains why, and is compelling reading for people of all faiths and none."
– General Sir Richard Dannatt, GCB CBE MC DL,
Chief of the General Staff 2006–2009

"I first met Andrew in Baghdad in 2003, where we both found ourselves under fire – physically and spiritually! I read the lesson at the church the day he re-opened it. Whilst in one sense he is no more or less than the rest of us – a man called by God to a task – he is nonetheless someone who has followed that call unremittingly. This eminently readable book tells his extraordinary story in a way that is typical of the man."
– Major General Tim Cross, CBE

www.lionhudson.com